"I have used **The Mindset for Winning** Mental Conditioning Program for five years and during that time our teams won 4 National Titles. The book offers a simple, complete, and extremely practical approach to mental training — and, most importantly, Dr. Curtis' techniques work with today's athletes. **The Mindset for Winning** is a must for coaches and athletes that want an edge on the competition."

Gary Wilson, Head Coach
Women's Track and Cross Country
University of Minnesota

"A very practical and readable approach to mental training that is quite useable by all athletes....just reading this book will improve performance."

Mark Hodges, Contributing Editor
Triathlete Magazine

"This is the most practical and complete book I've seen on the mental aspect of athletics. It's not only a valuable book for coaches and athletes, but I would recommend it for anyone who wants to be successful in any field."

Bill Bergan, Head Coach
Track and Cross Country
Iowa State University

"A valuable resource for athletes at all levels of competition — Olympic to Junior High School."

Terry Crawford, Head Coach
Women's Track and Cross Country
University of Texas
U.S. Women's Head Coach
1988 U.S. Olympic Team

"The ideas described in **The Mindset for Winning** helped me to excel at the college level and to make a smooth transition into professional athletics. These techniques can help you achieve things you thought were not attainable."

Tom Newberry
Los Angeles Rams
1986 NFL All-Rookie Team
1987 All-Madden Team
1988 NFL All-Pro Team

"No coach or serious athlete can expect to succeed without understanding the ideas and concepts contained in this book. It is, without a doubt, the best presentation on the subject of mental preparation and training I have read to date."

Brooks T. Johnson
Director of Track and Field
Stanford University
U.S. Women's Head Coach
1984 U.S. Olympic Team

THE MINDSET FOR

WINNING™

THE MINDSET FOR
WINNING

™

---

*A four-step mental training program
to achieve peak performance
for all athletes.*

JOHN D. CURTIS, Ph.D.

Coulee Press
La Crosse, Wisconsin

Manufactured in the United States of America

International Standard Book Number 0-9611456-3-3

Request for permissions should be addressed to:

COULEE PRESS
P.O. Box 1744
La Crosse, Wisconsin 54602-1744, USA
(608) 788-8464

To Kathy, my wife, and my children, Tim and Chad,
whom I love very much.

CONTENTS

INTRODUCTION

Coaches and athletes alike acknowledge that the outcome of sporting events does not necessarily favor the most skilled athletes — but it favors those that are mentally toughest on a given day. Yet, in spite of this fact, most athletes spend 90 to 95% of their time on the development of physical skills and very little time on the development of mental factors that lead to athletic success.

As I worked with athletes (from weekend golfers to professionals) over the years, I discovered they are more than willing to make the committment to improve their performance. However, it became apparent that most coaches and athletes do not have access to simple, understandable information for developing and implementing a mental training program that fits into one's schedule and lifestyle. As a result they spend their effort on that part of the program that they understand best, the physical side.

There are many excellent books available on the topic of mental training but they have one major weakness — the material is too difficult and/or too time consuming to properly implement in a successful format. Therefore, I wrote this book based on the Mental Conditioning Program that I have used with athletes for the past 15 years. **The Mindset for Winning** follows the same program used successfully by hundreds of athletes, from the high school level to the professional ranks, from weekend athletes to full-time athletes.

As you read through and follow the program, you too will find success as you use the powers of the mind to supplement and complement your physical training methods.

*"Whatever THE MIND OF MAN
can CONCEIVE and BELIEVE
it can ACHIEVE."*

NAPOLEON HILL
Author of *Think and Grow Rich*

PART I
THE FOUNDATION
OF THE PROGRAM

P art I of *The Mindset for Winning* defines the need for mental conditioning for athletes and examines various concepts upon which the program is based. The first three chapters cover the role of self-image and its importance in performance; the role the mind plays in your successes and failures in life; and the role of stress in performance as well as the need to control the stress in one's life to achieve optimal or peak performance. Lastly, Chapter 4 lists and discusses the benefits athletes can derive from learning and practicing relaxation techniques on a regular (daily) basis.

CHAPTER 1

THE SELF-IMAGE
AND PERFORMANCE

Preparation for Sports

Abraham Lincoln made the statement "If I had 8 hours to chop down a tree, I'd spend the first 6 hours sharpening the ax." In this quote Lincoln was referring to the importance of preparation. As athletes, we recognize the importance of preparation. We often develop detailed, well-thought-out plans and workout schedules to prepare for upcoming competitions. But are we preparing properly? All too often the answer is no!

In the quote above, Lincoln was referring to total preparation. To most efficiently chop down a tree, the ax must be sharpened on both sides. An ax sharpened on one side only can complete the job but not as easily and efficiently as a well-honed ax would do.

In athletics, outstanding performances involve the total athlete — mind and body. Proper preparation in both dimensions is required for optimum effort as well as optimum results. Could it be that we don't prepare properly to achieve desired results as often as we'd like?

In sports, too often we sharpen or hone just one side of the ax, the physical side. Often, 90% or more of an athlete's training program addresses this physical dimension with little or no time spent on the mental dimension. Yet, most athletes as well as coaches accept the idea that, all things being equal, the team or person best prepared mentally will win.

To consistently achieve high level performances, we must balance our preparation. We must do more for mental preparation than reminding ourselves to "get ready mentally" or "concentrate" on our performance. To truly reach our top level of performance on a regular basis, we must learn to prepare ourselves mentally and then follow through with that preparation. Greater knowledge and time and effort in mental preparation will reward us with improved performance.

Why Mental Preparation?

All athletes create images in their minds prior to engaging in an event — and the images that are conjured up can create a problem. Too often the images are negative ones which may lead to anxiety, low self-image, poor attitude and expectations, and less than desired behaviors and performances. The purpose of mental preparation for athletes is to change negative thought processes to positive thought processes which will establish positive expectations prior to engaging in an athletic event.

This is not to suggest that mental preparation is a "cure all" and will guarantee improved performance. However, positive mental preparation will increase or enhance the possibilities of doing well or improving performance. In addition, some researchers believe that some of the benefits achieved from mental preparation may be explained by motivational factors. An athlete willing to put more time and effort into a sport is likely to be more motivated to succeed than one who only practices physically.

THE SELF-IMAGE CYCLE

The success we achieve in an event is directly related to the attitudes and expectations we carry into that event. Psychological research supports the premise that "we are what we think about." Our self-image is determined by the thoughts and visualizations that we hold in our minds, both consciously and unconsciously. Self-image affects our attitudes, expectations, behaviors, and performances in all areas of our lives (See Figure 1-1).

FIGURE 1-1

THE SELF-IMAGE CYCLE

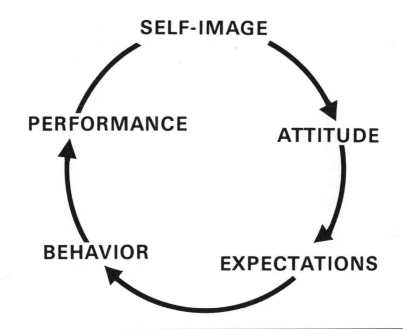

Our self-image is like a blueprint that determines our behaviors. If an athlete has a poor self-image or holds negative thoughts and images in his/her mind, the behavior will support this negative image and poor performances as well as poor attitudes will result.

Conversely, an athlete with a positive self-image and positive expectations will support that image with positive performances.

TEAM IMAGE

Interestingly enough, whole teams can pick up on this image (either positive or negative) and we see corresponding behaviors and performances.

Vince Lombardi, considered by many to be one of the greatest coaches of all time because of his ability to get the most effort from his players, recognized this power of the mind. His most famous quote was "winning isn't everything, but the will to win is everything." His greatness as a coach was his ability to convey this "will to win" to his players on a team basis. This resulted in a positive "team-image" (similar to self-image but on a team basis) in his players which was reflected in their performances. This in turn reinforced the positive team image.

THE SUCCESS CYCLE

When this self-image cycle is positive, we find that positive performances reinforce positive self-image, which helps establish positive attitudes and expectations. These, in turn, result in improved behaviors that lead to improved performances. Eventually this positive cycle of success leads individuals (as well as teams) to a new attitude — They EXPECT TO WIN, RATHER THAN HOPE TO WIN. This is the thinking developed by true champions in all walks of life.

FIGURE 1-2

THE SUCCESS CYCLE

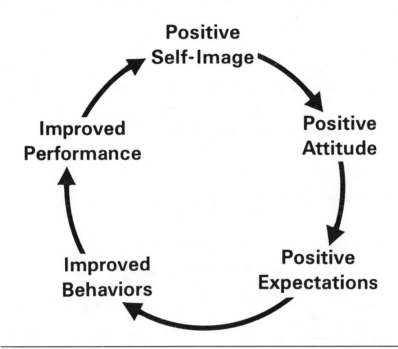

Positive Self-Image → Positive Attitude → Positive Expectations → Improved Behaviors → Improved Performance → Positive Self-Image

This winning mindset (i.e., expecting to win or do well) is the backbone of sports dynasties. It's often called tradition. A winning tradition is simply a "thinking process" ingrained in team members because of continual success. New members of a team pick up these positive expectations from veteran members, which correspond with positive performances, which reinforce self/team-image.

THE FAILURE CYCLE

Conversely, negative self-image contributes to a negative attitude and negative expectations which lead to negative behaviors that result in poorer performances. These reinforce the negative self-image which keeps the cycle going in a failure mode.

It is the thinking process or, more accurately, the self-image cycle, which explains why some individuals or teams always do well, why some are average, and why some are viewed as losers.

FIGURE 1-3

THE FAILURE CYCLE

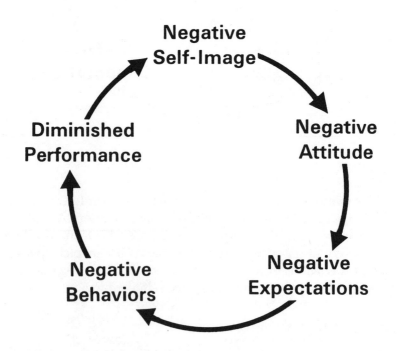

Altering Self-Image

We can alter an individual or team performance by intervening in the self-image cycle illustrated in Figure 1-1. To do so, we must determine the images — the true images — that are held in one's mind. Then, we must create new visualizations to replace the negative ones that are having a detrimental impact on our self-image. If we alter our self-image, we alter the corresponding attitudes, expectations, behaviors, and performance.

If a mental conditioning program is implemented properly, changes can take place very quickly. I have seen athletes change their negative self-image to a positive one literally overnight while others require weeks of work to alter the self-image.

Several years ago I was asked to work with a high school baseball team which had a 6-10 overall record (2-8 and last place in their conference). The coach realized that the athletes displayed good physical skills in practice but played poorly in games. Their next game was 8 days off. Their opponent would be a team that had just won the conference title, was 13-3, had already beaten them twice, and was ranked second in the state. The goal of both the coach and the athletes was to beat this team in the regional tournament.

The team began the "Condensed" program (outlined in Chapter 9) because of the time-line. The athletes practiced the program 6 to 8 times daily. The coach noted that within three days the athletes displayed more positive behavior at practice. The athletes began to believe they could win the game and, by the day of the game, they expected to win. They played their best game of the year and entered the last inning behind 6-5. In the top of the last inning their opponents scored 3 runs to take a 9-5 lead. Yet, as they came to bat there was the positive feeling in the dugout that they could still win the game. With two out and nobody on, a rally started that didn't end until the game was won 10-9. Immediately after the game the athletes started saying "We can go to state, we already beat the number two ranked team." (This game was the first round of the state tournament.) They took a 7-10 record into the first sectional game and beat a team with a 14-3 record by a score of 3-2. They won the sectional finals with a 3-0 win over a team with a 14-5 record and advanced to the state tournament. They became the second team in the history of the state tournament to advance to the tournament with a losing record (9-10).

In the first game of the state tournament they beat a 17-3 team by a 1-0 score and were not defeated until the semi-finals, thus finishing the season with a 10-11 record. By altering their self-image, these athletes altered their team-image, their attitude and expectations which changed their behavior in practice. Their positive performances reinforced the new self-image/team-image to complete the success cycle. This entire process literally took place over a period of days.

Positive changes in individuals and teams are not a rare occurrence. I have seen it happen time and time again. The results I have encountered are consistent with those reported in the literature on self-image and visualization for improved performances. However, the key to improved performance through a mental training program is to understanding why mental training works. Then the program can be implemented properly.

This book offers a hands-on, practical program for you, the athlete. As such, I will focus on how to properly implement a mental conditioning program rather than on the research which supports the use of visualizations and imagery for improved performance. Regardless of whether you are a weekend golfer, a high school, college, or professional athlete, the strategies outlined in this book can and will have a major impact on your success if followed as recommended.

CHAPTER 2
THE MIND RULES THE BODY

T he underlying principle behind mental practice, and, indeed, all successes and failures in our lives has to do with the fact that the mind rules the body. We've all been introduced to this concept before, but most people don't understand the power of the mind/body relationship. To be successful in implementing a mental conditioning program it is imperative that you understand the mind/body connection and recognize that you perform consistently with your self-image. The first step to altering performance is to alter the self-image.

Hypnosis Versus De-hypnosis

HYPNOSIS

A basic fact of the mind/body relationship is that each of us is hypnotized right at this moment. We've been hypnotized by ourselves and others to believe that certain things are true. If we believe these things to be true, even if they aren't, we act as if they are true and we perform as if they are true. The beliefs that we hold to be true are the basis of our self-image.

Let's look at some examples of how we've allowed ourselves to become hypnotized. How are you in mathematics? Good, average, poor? How about spelling? How "mechanically inclined" are you? How good at public speaking are you? Does speaking to a large group of people cause you stress? Do you come through "in the pinch" on a regular basis when the pressure is on you? Are you accident prone?

We all hold certain beliefs about ourselves. These positive and negative beliefs are the basis of our self-image. They are a result of our past experiences which include our thoughts, comments made by others, our past performances, and the like that we have accepted as being true. As an example, many people believe they are poor in mathematics (or some other subject), yet they may be outstanding in all other subjects. How do we develop these thoughts or beliefs that limit us? I'll use mathematics as the example since I was "bad" in math for years yet was average to above average in all other subjects. I remember my parents telling my older sister after she received her report card, "Don't worry, we're all bad in math." I subconsciously accepted the fact that members of our family while good in other subjects, were unable to comprehend mathematics.

When I started school I knew I'd be poor in mathematics (remember, the foundation for this belief was laid earlier and I'd accepted it). As a result I didn't look forward to math class, I didn't put much effort into assignments and studying, and my poor grades reconfirmed that I was poor in math. This is the Self-image cycle at work in a negative way (Figure 1-3).

I was placed in a group with other students that were poor in math. Everyone knew which group was the smartest, which was average and which group included poor-achieving students. My placement with the poor math group reinforced my self-image. Since we always perform consistently with our self-image, for years I performed poorly in mathematics as I fulfilled my self-image. I remained poor in math until I applied the principles found in this book to my studies in math and related subjects.

We've all done this to ourselves, or allowed others to do it to us (but remember, they can only do it with our approval). This same concept carries over to sports. That's why some athletes are "great" in practice but perform poorly in games or vice versa. It's why Reggie Jackson is called "Mr. October." After doing well during several Octobers, the newspapers labeled him Mr. October. Soon opposing pitchers became stressful when they faced him. People forget that he strikes out and has had poor games in October, like others fortunate enough to make it to the World Series. Because of his reputation most sports fans just remember and focus on his positive exploits in October. Remember the self-image cycle from Chapter 1?

Although hypnotists disagree on both the definition and the precise nature of hypnosis, all would agree that hypnosis involves giving suggestions. While in a trance (sometimes without a trance), once a suggestion is accepted by the mind as being true the body responds accordingly. Under hypnosis, if a subject sitting in a warm room (70°F) is told that they are in a cold room with inadequate clothing, they are likely to begin shivering. If they are told they are in a hot, humid, tropical climate, they may begin to sweat. It has also been reported that subjects developed blisters when told that the hypnotist's finger was a hot poker and the hypnotist touched them with that finger.

Hypnosis has been used effectively to block out pain during surgery, childbirth, removal of teeth, and severe headaches. It has also been used to remove warts, to stop internal bleeding, and to slow bleeding of certain body parts during surgery. In each of these examples, people respond physically to images they accept as being true in their mind.

DE-HYPNOSIS

What actually happens during hypnosis would be more accurately described as de-hypnosis. Hypnosis does not add to the body's ability to do something; rather, it removes the barriers or limitations we, as individuals, have placed on ourselves or allowed others to place on us.

I'll use an example of a man who can bench press 130 pounds to illustrate this point. One hundred thirty pounds is his absolute maximum. If 132 pounds are placed on the bar, he can't bench press it. While in a hypnotic state, he is told to bench press 140 pounds. He proceeds to bench press 140 pounds several times. Why can he do it while hypnotized and not be able to do it in a non-hypnotized state?

If the man can do 140 pounds while hypnotized, that means that 140 pounds is within his physiological limits. If 143 pounds is outside his physiological limit he will not be able to bench press that weight even if he is hypnotised. What hypnosis did was remove the "mental barrier" of 130 pounds placed there because of previous experiences. When that barrier was removed, he could perform up to his physiological limit of 140 pounds.

So the term de-hypnosis would be more accurate when describing what currently is thought of as hypnosis. De-hypnosis means removing the mental barriers that limit our performance.

In sports, as in life, we have placed "mental barriers" that prevent us from performing at our maximum. What we need to do is to remove these barriers. To establish the mindset for winning, we must first alter our self-image and our performance level will be affected accordingly.

The Mind/Body Relationship

I've discovered that to be successful with mental conditioning you must do more than know there is a mind/body relationship, you must actually understand this relationship. In this section I'll give examples to illustrate this relationship. I selected the examples presented here because they lay an excellent base of understanding for the upcoming program.

MIND/BODY CONNECTION
EXAMPLE 1: ULCERS

Most people are familiar with the physical condition called ulcers and recognize that the mind — through stress and worries — contributes to this condition. To really understand the power of the mind, remember that your mind is so strong and affects your body to such an extent that the mind can actually eat a hole in your stomach. Now that's a powerful relationship! Through worry, the mind can cause the body to release various chemicals that throw off the homeostatic balance of the body and cause a disruptive influence on our health. This imbalance of chemicals can allow enzymes to eat through the walls of our stomachs causing ulcers. Interestingly enough, if a person with ulcers regains control of their thinking process and alters their attitude toward life, they can often heal the ulcers — again showing the power of the mind.

MIND/BODY CONNECTION
EXAMPLE 2: JOGGER/MUGGER

Imagine that you are walking alone late at night in an area in which a person was attacked several nights previously. The street lights are broken and the area is dark. As you walk by a row of shrubs you hear someone running quietly up behind you. How do you react?

If you think "mugger," the body sets off the stress response (often called the fight-or-flight response). Physiologically, you respond with an increased heart rate, increased breathing rate, increased blood pressure, increased cardiac output and decreased blood clotting time, all of which are designed to prepare you to respond to this stressful situation.

However, if you think "jogger" when you hear the footsteps behind you, you do not respond physiologically, simply because your perception of the situation is different. You may or may not look backwards and may even move to the side to allow the "jogger" to run by.

In both instances, the body is responding to our mind, our thought process. Although the circumstances are exactly the same, if we think "mugger" we respond physiologically one way and if we think "jogger" we respond physiologically in a different way.

Can you think of a similiar experience that happened to you that would illustrate the mind/body connection? Think of a time when your mind set off the stress response inappropriately. For example, did you ever see a coat or a robe hanging from a door at night and think a person was behind the door; or hear a noise that caused you to think someone was breaking into your house (causing the stress response to be set off) when in fact, the noise was a furnace, the wind, or a radio?

MIND/BODY CONNECTION
EXAMPLE 3: THE LEMON TEST

First read through the following paragraphs. Then sit quietly, close your eyes, and imagine the exercise listed below. As you visualize the exercise, be sure to visualize it from within your own eyes, as if you are actually doing it.

Description:

Close your eyes, and imagine a large, juicy, yellow lemon sitting on a table with a knife lying next to it. Walk over to the table, pick up the knife, and cut the lemon in half..........then cut it into quarters......

Picture the lemon as you pick up one of the quarters and examine it in detail.....

Notice the yellow "meat" of the lemon.....and the rind.....and feel the coolness of the rind in your fingers.....

Squeeze the lemon in your hand and notice the juice coming to the surface.....

Now, see the lemon as you move it to your mouth.....and bite down on the meat of the lemon as you squeeze some of the juice into your mouth.....

Taste the sourness.....the bitterness of the juice in your mouth......

Feel.....taste.....and experience the sour juice in your mouth...

And then open your eyes.

The Lemon Test illustrates the mind/body relationship because most people will experience salivation when they close their eyes and visualize themselves biting down on a lemon. In fact, just reading the description of the exercise may have caused you to salivate without even closing the eyes and "seeing it." This illustrates that our bodies can respond to word symbols as well as to visual symbols. That's important to remember when we move into Chapter 6, when we discuss Positive Affirmation Statements.

MIND/BODY CONNECTION
EXAMPLE 4: CHEVREUL'S PENDULUM

Perhaps the most fascinating and graphic illustration of the mind/body connection is Chevreul's Pendulum. This technique not only illustrates the mind/body connection but it also illustrates why mental practice works to improve physical skills.

Materials Needed

For this technique, you will need a pendulum. You can make your own pendulum by tying a ring to a string or tying a paper clip to a thread.

Description

Sit in a chair and grasp the pendulum between your thumb and forefinger of your dominant hand. Rest your elbow on your leg with the pendulum hanging down about ten inches from your hand (see Figure 2-1).

FIGURE 2-1

POSITION FOR CHEVREUL'S PENDULUM

While keeping your eyes open and watching the pendulum, focus your attention on the exhalation phase of your breathing rhythm and allow your body to relax......

Watch the pendulum closely and remain relaxed, but picture in your own mind the pendulum swinging freely toward you and away from you (from A to B in Figure 2-2) .....after 10 to 20 seconds the pendulum will begin to swing in this direction without you consciously moving it......

FIGURE 2-2

CHEVREUL'S PENDULUM

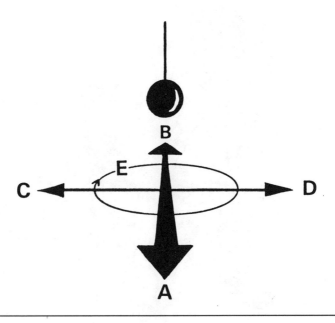

Now imagine or visualize the pendulum changing directions and swinging from side to side (from C to D in Figure 2-2).....visualize this in your mind (with the eyes open and watching the pendulum) until the pendulum begins moving in this direction.

After it's swinging freely in this direction, imagine it moving in a circle in a clockwise direction until the pendulum moves in the circle.....

Then take a deep breath, and flex and stretch as you complete the exercise.

When doing Chevreul's pendulum, the pendulum changes directions as you visualize the change yet you are not consciously making it move. What is actually taking place is an unconscious response which is called subliminal motor movement. The muscles of the arm are contracting in the same sequence as if you are consciously moving the pendulum. But what is actually happening is happening on a subconscious level. You are thinking about the movement — and visualizing it — but the movements are taking place on a subliminal level which is too minor to perceive. The hand and fingers may not be moving enough to be seen. However, the length of the pendulum chain magnifies the movement so we can see it.

When doing mental practice to improve a specific skill such as a golf swing or a tennis serve, you are imprinting the mind, the nervous system and the muscular system with the proper blueprint of how to do the skill. As long as you visualize the movement from your own eyes — from within — and feel what is taking place within the body as well as visualize the end result such as the ball following the perfect flight, the body will actually perform the exact motions needed to achieve the end result; but the body will do so on a subliminal level.

CHAPTER 3
THE ROLE OF STRESS
IN PERFORMANCE

A characteristic of high level performers is that they control the level of stress in their bodies — they are not controlled by the stress. This is not to say that stress and tensions are negative. In fact, stress is a normal, desirable, beneficial part of our lives. Most people are more active, more invigorated, more creative, more productive, in general, more alive because of stress. Therefore, stress is not something to be avoided, but it is a state we must understand and control if we are to fully appreciate and profit from it during an athletic contest. To fully understand and appreciate the stress response of the body, we must understand why the stress response is so vital and necessary in our lives.

The stress response is designed to help us deal with life-threatening situations. It is a physical preparation of the body that increases our chances of survival. For example, when one of our ancestors encountered a dangerous animal, his body would respond almost instantly to prepare him for the physical fight with the animal or the physical flight from it. Hence, the stress response has been dubbed the "fight or flight" response.

What is important to understand is that the physical reactions of the body that take place when one is under stress are designed to

action, to get it geared up for the physical fight
.ne danger. These physical reactions include, but
, the following:

   .d sympathetic nervous system activity (the portion of
   .rvous system that prepares one for action)
- . .eased body metabolism
  Increased heart rate
  Increased blood pressure
  Increased breathing rate
  Increased oxygen consumption
  Increased cardiac output
- Increased muscular tension
- Decreased blood clotting time (to help ensure survival if injured)
- Increased blood flow to the major muscle groups involved in the fight or flight (including the chest for breathing, and the arms and legs for fighting, kicking and running)
- Increased mental activity
- Decreased perception of fatigue

As a result of the physiological changes that take place during the stress response, most athletes perform better when under stress than they do without stress. The key is being under the proper amount of stress — not too much, not too little. If a person is too relaxed the performance will suffer as will the performance of an athlete under too much stress. To illustrate this point, I'll examine Figure 3-1, the performance curve. (See next page.)

In Figure 3-1, the dotted line represents an athlete's performance. Notice that as the tension level (level of stress) increases, the athlete's performance increases as well, until it reaches the tension level represented by point A. At this tension level, the performance level peaks (point B, the upper point on the dotted line). Point A is the ideal tension level for a particular athlete in a particular sport in order to achieve "maximum" or "peak" performance. Ideal tension level varies; it would be different for a golfer versus a football player, and it would be different from individual to individual within the same sport.

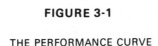

FIGURE 3-1

THE PERFORMANCE CURVE

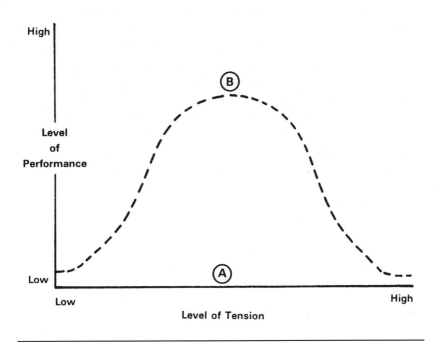

If the athlete experiences increased tension beyond point A on the baseline, performance level diminishes. The higher the tension level moves beyond point A, the lower the performance level becomes. This diminished performance is illustrated by the downward movement of the dotted line.

In athletic circles, the common term for this decreased performance due to too much stress is "choking." The term choking comes from a Greek term which literally means a narrowing of the esophagus, or to choke. When a person is under too much stress the esophagus actually does constrict or narrow.

When an athlete experiences too high a stress level, such as when moving beyond point A, the muscles get too tense. The athlete no longer allows the performance to happen as trained to do during practice sessions. At this point athletes are too excited and tend to force things to happen or are unable to respond at all. The missed two-foot putt in golf or the missed lay-up at the buzzer are examples of forcing things because of too much stress. Watching a called third strike with the tying run on third base in the last inning would be an example of being unable to respond due to too much stress. In each case, too much stress hindered optimal performance regardless of the sport.

It is important to realize then, that stress is needed if we are to achieve optimal performance. But equally important is the ability to control our level of stress so that it does not become extreme and hinder performance on the other end. The goal for optimal performance is to realize when we have too little or too much stress and to be able to alter our arousal level accordingly.

CHAPTER 4
THE BENEFITS OF RELAXATION FOR ATHLETES

In pressure situations, most average athletes tend to get too aroused, or too stressed. This is why they remain average athletes and do not get the maximum from their abilities. To achieve optimum performance on a regular basis, the ability to relax and control this tendency to become over-aroused is necessary. But relaxation is more important to peak performance than just to control this over-arousal state. The benefits of relaxation for athletes as well as for non-athletes are numerous. Listed below are some of the major benefits an athlete will derive from the ability to relax. This chapter will examine each of these benefits and discuss how each can contribute to improved performance.

The major benefits of relaxation for athletes are:

Relaxation prepares one for mental imagery.
Relaxation improves concentration ability.
Relaxation helps control arousal level.
Relaxation helps one sleep better.
Relaxation helps improve body awareness.

Relaxation reduces recovery time.
Relaxation decreases minor illnesses and symptoms of illness.
Relaxation increases sociability.

The Benefits of Relaxation for Athletes

RELAXATION PREPARES ONE FOR MENTAL IMAGERY

As we move through life we view things as they currently are. The rational mind, which is the conscious mind, views things as we know them to be. If we try to alter this image, the rational mind fights this new image. For example, I was working with an athlete whose best high jump was 6' 6". I asked him to imagine himself jumping 6' 10", which was a height that his coach knew he was capable of jumping. The athlete actually started laughing because his rational mind knew that this was not the way things were at the time. He had jumped 6' 6" and that was the image the rational mind could accept.

The rational mind is great for "arguing for our limitations." I see this all the time when working with athletes. In the example above the young man's rational mind was probably saying something like "this guy is crazy, he knows your best jump is 6' 6". What you should be doing is concentrating on jumping 6' 7" — or on jumping 6' 6" again. You know you only did it once." The rational mind likes the status quo; it feels comfortable with the way things currently are.

To improve your performance, you must alter your image or perception of yourself. Remember, we always act and behave consistent with our self image. If we see ourselves as a 6' 6" jumper, we'll never jump higher unless we see the potential for jumping higher. To alter our image we need to send new thoughts and visualizations to our brain. But to do this successfully we have to overcome the rational mind which likes things just the way they are.

Relaxation is the technique used to shut down the rational mind so that we can feed "new" visualizations and ideas into the brain and do so with conviction. When the rational mind is slowed down or shut down via relaxation, the new images we imagine are fed directly to our subconscious and accepted as real. Remember the body cannot tell the difference between a real and an imagined experience.

The high jumper used relaxation to shut down the rational mind. When in the relaxed state he was able to visualize the 6' 10" jump; before the season ended, he jumped 6' 10".

FIGURE 4-1

LEVELS OF ALERTNESS

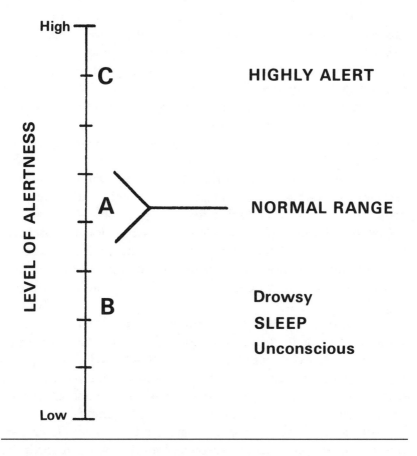

Figure 4-1 represents various levels of alertness we can experience. We spend most of our time within the normal range (A in Figure 4-1).

At various times throughout the day we may dip to low levels and become tired and sleepy (B in Figure 4-1). At other times we may experience high levels of alertness (C in Figure 4-1) where the mind is highly focused, such as during an athletic contest.

At point C the mind is focused and alert. It is difficult to break an athlete's concentration at this level. At this point the athlete is in control of his/her consciousness. The crowd noise and movement will not interrupt a highly skilled athlete. If a member of the crowd were to yell "Fire!" during a time when the athlete is highly focused, the athlete would not hear the noise since it would be blocked out.

Yet, later in the evening, if the same athlete were to become drowsy or fall asleep (B in Figure 4-1), and if someone yelled "Fire! Get out of the house it's on fire!" the athlete would probably react, even if there were no fire. When in this state of lowered alertness, the athlete is reacting to a suggestion which is being fed directly into the unconscious mind without the assessment of the rational mind to check out the message. Once we become more alert, the rational mind would analyze the situation and check to see if there is smoke, if others are reacting, etc.

The point is, our level of consciousness affects our acceptance or rejection of the power of suggestion. In a highly alert state, the conscious mind may be highly focused and not even "hear" the suggestion. During normal levels of alertness the rational mind checks the message out and determines whether to accept it or reject it. At levels of lower consciousness, the rational mind is shut down, or at least slowed down, and the subconscious mind is more likely to accept suggestion.

This is the reason why relaxation is so important as the base or the foundation of the mental conditioning program. Relaxation helps lower our level of consciousness and thus slows down or shuts down the rational mind. At this point, while in the relaxed state, the unconscious mind can be fed the new visualizations without argument or outright rejection by the conscious mind.

Although this first benefit of relaxation for athletes (To prepare one for imagery) is the prime reason for introducing relaxation in the mental conditioning program, there are many other benefits that an athlete can derive from performing and perfecting relaxation.

RELAXATION IMPROVES CONCENTRATION ABILITY

Relaxation training can help both intensity and duration of one's concentration. There are several reasons why relaxation training is excellent training for improved concentration. First, to successfully perform a relaxation technique, you must learn to focus your attention as well as learn to tune-out distractions. Second, as you become deeply relaxed, it would be easy to drift off into a state of sleep; it requires concentration to prevent this from happening. Third, many techniques require intense focusing of attention within the body to feel sensations that are often difficult to isolate and feel. In each of these cases you must concentrate to become successful.

Not only is this improved ability to concentrate important in athletics, it also has tremendous carry-over value to other areas of one's life. Relaxation is often used to improve concentration for people in various work settings. I've had good success using it with students who had difficulty studying due to a wandering mind.

Although most relaxation techniques help improve the intensity and duration of concentration to some degree, some techniques and exercises are better than others if improved concentration is a major goal. Specific techniques beneficial in improving concentration will be discussed in Chapter 10.

RELAXATION HELPS CONTROL AROUSAL LEVEL

Research done on relaxation indicates that people who relax regularly have better control over their physical and psychological arousal levels than do individuals who do not relax regularly. If a person relaxes, there is less tendency to over-react to stressful situations. Those who relax regularly are also able to "come down" from stress faster than do people that do not relax regularly.

In addition, as mentioned earlier, it is important for athletes to be able to determine the best arousal level for maximum performance. When you near the arousal level that results in "peak performance," short relaxation techniques and breathing skills can be helpful in preventing the arousal level from continuing to increase which could result in diminished performance.

RELAXATION HELPS ONE SLEEP BETTER

As you learn to relax effectively, you gain better control over your thoughts through the increased ability to concentrate. This allows you to "tune out" thoughts when it's time to sleep and to fall asleep more easily. This is important for good health and can be extremely beneficial for athletes on nights prior to important athletic events.

In addition, during relaxation, physiological and psychological arousal decreases and tension diminishes. This reduced arousal level carries over to the sleeping state and the body can "rejuvenate" more quickly than when the body is tense during sleep. It is common for people who relax regularly to report sleeping 1/2 hour to 2 hours less per night than they did prior to practicing relaxation on a regular basis.

RELAXATION HELPS IMPROVE BODY AWARENESS

During many relaxation techniques, as we focus our attention within the body, we learn better sensory awareness. Sensory awareness is an increased consciousness of sensory perceptions and sensations. Increased sensory awareness means that messages from the body as well as general feelings become perceived at a conscious level. In essence, we learn to tune into such messages as tension, relaxation, pressure, temperature change, movement, stillness as well as vague feelings such as happiness, peace, contentment, patience, comfort, anger, or frustration. This increased sensory awareness leads to improved body awareness, or a better understanding as to what's taking place within the body.

Improved body awareness allows the athlete to "monitor" his/her body better during practice and sporting events. For example, a distance runner can monitor her body during the race and thus learn to run "at the edge" or "within herself" — to exert the proper energy and speed to attain maximum performance throughout the race. A golfer who notices too much tension can do a basic breathing technique to bring the tension level down to an acceptable level for maximum performance.

In addition, in most sports, kinisthetic sense is important to improve the feel of one's movements and actions. Improved sensory awareness helps athletes tune into their kinisthetic senses, which gives them a better "feel" for the movements as they are performing.

RELAXATION REDUCES RECOVERY TIME

After physical exertion, whether it is a strenuous practice or a competitive game, the body needs to recover if the athlete is going to perform at optimal level in the near future. During physical exertion waste products build-up in the muscles. These waste products are removed as blood comes into an area to "cleanse it." They should be removed as soon as possible.

Improved circulation (blood flow) not only reduces recovery time following a workout but also reduces healing time following an injury. Usually, the better the blood flow to an injured area, the faster the healing.

Relaxation improves blood flow to various body parts, including the arms and legs. Individuals can learn to warm an area through biofeedback and/or sensory feedback (being able to feel the warmth in an area) and can learn to direct blood flow to a group of muscles to remove the waste product build-up.

After a workout or competition, when the body is cooled down properly, deep relaxation can give you the edge over your competitors by increasing blood flow to the fatigued muscles to remove waste products which have built up. I especially recommend this for sports that require intense physical exertion (i.e., endurance events, football, basketball, soccer, etc.) or between heats during track and field events.

RELAXATION CAN DECREASE MINOR ILLNESSES AND SYMPTOMS OF ILLNESS

Research indicates that people who relax on a regular basis have fewer symptoms of illness as well as less actual illnesses. When a person is under stress, it is speculated that the immune system wears down so the body has less resistance to minor illnesses, such as colds or the flu, as well as to flare-ups of stress-related problems unique to the individual. Figure 4-2 lists some illnesses that are directly or indirectly related to stress. (See next page.)

This point has increased significance for an athlete. As a sport season progresses, workouts and competitions intensify so an athlete will "peak" for tournament play. This increased intensity can lead to greater stress for the athlete. In the school setting, mid-term and final exams often coincide with times of increased stress in sports. During

FIGURE 4-2

STRESS RELATED HEALTH PROBLEMS

Depression	Ulcerative colitis
Coronary heart disease	Gout
Peptic ulcer	Cancer
Asthma	Skin rashes
Diabetes	Accidents
Lower back pain	Multiple sclerosis
Headaches	Mental health problems
High blood pressure	Family violence
Arthritis	Child abuse
Spastic bowel	Suicide

these high stress periods athletes are most susceptible to stress-related health problems which can hinder performance just when the best performances of the season are needed.

It is precisely at these "high stress periods" that I recommend extra relaxation, adequate sleep, and a balanced diet which emphasizes foods rich in B complex vitamins, vitamin A, and vitamin C. And, since the body requires extra vitamin C during stressful periods, I occasionally recommend a vitamin C tablet to be on the safe side.

RELAXATION INCREASES SOCIABILITY

Those who relax on a regular basis score higher on scales of sociability than those who do not relax regularly.

In many sports, your ability to get along with the coach, teammates, and significant others in your life (i.e., parents, siblings, roommates, boyfriend/girlfriend, spouse, etc.) affects your attitude toward yourself and your teammates. A positive attitude usually results in greater team cohesiveness and overall improved performance.

"The power to move the world is in your subconscious mind."

WILLIAM JAMES
Father of American Psychology

PART II
THE MENTAL CONDITIONING PROGRAM

Part I laid the base for the use of mental conditioning in athletics. Part II presents the actual Mental Conditioning Program. The four basic steps of the Mental Conditioning Program are introduced in the sequence in which they should be learned.

They are: (1) Relaxation — shutting down the rational mind; (2) Positive Affirmation Statements — preparing the mind for the upcoming visualizations; (3) Mental Recall — "convincing" the body that it can achieve optimal performances both mentally and physically because you've already done it at times in the past; and, (4) Mental Rehearsal — visualizing a future performance to accomplish a sought after goal.

CHAPTER 5
STEP ONE
RELAXATION

Being able to relax and performing relaxation on a regular basis can provide athletes with a variety of benefits that enhance performance. This chapter will focus on the benefit most important for the Mental Conditioning Program — relaxation prepares you for mental imagery.

The role that relaxation plays in preparing you for Mental Conditioning was previously discussed. What is most important to remember is that relaxation prepares the athlete for mental conditioning by shutting down the rational mind which is the part of the mind which sees things as they currently are. The rational mind is also that part of the mind which argues for your limitations.

During relaxation, when the rational mind is slowed down or shut down, you can present mental pictures of your "new self" directly to the subconscious mind. The subconscious more readily accepts these pictures while you are in the relaxed state. If this is done on a regular basis, the blueprints in our mind can be altered which can alter your self-image, your attitude, and your behavior as well as your performance.

The purpose of this chapter is simply to present two relaxation techniques. These techniques were selected because: they are easy to learn; they can be perfected in a short period of time; and, they lay the base for techniques to be presented in Chapter 10, which can be used during competition for controlling arousal, for relaxing, for physical recovery or to regain concentration, whichever is needed.

The Breathing Rhythms

To most effectively learn basic relaxation skills, an understanding of the breathing rhythms and their use in relaxation is important. The breathing cycle has two distinct phases, the inhalation phase and the exhalation phase.

INHALATION PHASE

The inhalation phase of the breathing cycle is the invigoration or tension-producing phase. When performing relaxation skills, obviously you do not want to produce tension. However, the inhalation portion of the breathing cycle is important in reversing the relaxed state and is used to come out of the relaxed state. When ready to end an exercise, a deep breath or two should be taken. This deep inhalation will create tension and help bring you back to your normal level of alertness. Somewhat like a yawn, deep inhalation is usually combined with the flexing and stretching of muscles much like one does when awakening from a state of sleep.

EXHALATION PHASE

The exhalation phase of the breathing cycle is the relaxation phase. If attention is focused on the exhalation phase, a feeling of sinking down, slowing down, heaviness, and in general a feeling of relaxation is felt. These sensations (sinking down, slowing down, heaviness, and general relaxation), when felt during the exhalation phase of the breathing cycle, will carry you into a state of relaxation.

Using the Breathing Rhythms to Relax

The basic techniques in this book all use the exhalation phase of the breathing cycle to achieve a feeling of relaxation. To perform each of these techniques, you must remember and follow four basic criteria.

1. Breathe normally. Observe the breathing cycle passively. In other words, let your body breathe by itself and quietly observe yourself breathe just as if you were a bystander.

2. Disregard the inhalations. **Do not** think about the inhalations at all. Just permit your body to inhale by itself without any conscious thought on your part.

3. Focus your attention on the exhalation phase of the breathing cycle. Concentrate and think about the exhalations.

4. Feel and experience key sensations as you exhale. The sensations you may notice are sinking down, slowing down, heaviness, and an overall letting go or feeling of relaxation. **The key to the breathing rhythms is to feel the sensations as you exhale — and only as you exhale. To enhance the relaxation effect, you must synchronize the key feeling with the exhalation phase.**

NOTE: Words that are hyphenated letter-by-letter (e.g., s-i-n-k-i-n-g d-o-w-n) should be repeated slowly in your mind in time with the exhalation phase of your breathing cycle.

Periods (...) indicate a pause. The length of the pause is determined by the number of periods used. The more periods, the longer the pause (i.e., ... is twice as long as ....).

EXERCISE ONE
THE EXHALATION EXERCISE

Description

The exhalation exercise will establish the exhalation phase of your breathing cycle as the cue for relaxation to occur within your body. It will establish the ground rules for the second exercise. As you perform this exercise remember to (1) breathe normally; (2) disregard the inhalations; (3) focus your attention on the exhalation phase of the breathing cycle; and (4) feel, sense and experience the key sensations as you exhale.

Directions

Assume a comfortable relaxation position with as much support as possible. Do not cross the arms or legs. During this exercise, be sure to maintain a passive attitude and to allow relaxation to occur.

When ready, allow yourself to close your eyes and, for the first several (e.g., two to five) breathing cycles, quietly observe the air as it enters and leaves your nose.....................

Now, for the next several breaths, focus only on the exhalation phase of the breathing cycle, notice the warmth of the air as it leaves your nose and r-e-l-a-x as you exhale..........and r-e-l-a-x as you exhale..........and allow yourself to l-e-t g-o as you continue to focus on your exhalations..........................and r-e-l-a-x as you exhale ....and r-e-l-a-x as you exhale...............................

Now, as you exhale, feel or sense the body s-i-n-k-i-n-g d-o-w-n into the supporting environment...

Notice the body sinking d-o-w-n..........and d-o-w-n, more and more with each exhalation...............................

At this time, as you exhale, feel the body s-l-o-w-i-n-g d-o-w-n ....You may notice the breathing rhythm slowing down, or possibly the heart beat slowing down........., or possibly just an overall sense of patience.........Each time you notice any of these sensations, allow the body to let go and relax more and more..........letting go, sinking down, and r-e-l-a-x-i-n-g..............................

Now, remain in the relaxed state for several moments............. and, when ready to end the relaxation, take a deep breath as you flex, stretch, and open your eyes.

EXERCISE TWO
THE SEQUENTIAL RELAXATION EXERCISE

The second phase of the deep relaxation program to prepare you for the mental conditioning is the sequential relaxation exercise which incorporates the exhalation exercise with relaxation of specific body parts. This is done in a sequential manner throughout the body, thus the name sequential relaxation.

Description

Sequential relaxation will use the exhalation phase of the breathing rhythm to allow specific body parts to relax. When the sensation of relaxation develops in a body part, attention will be moved to another body part until that one is relaxed. This is continued until total body relaxation is achieved. To perform this exercise, you should follow the criteria listed below:

1. Focus your attention on a specific body part. Although it is not essential, for the sake of simplicity it is recommended that you use the following sequence:
> foot; lower leg (calf region); upper leg (thigh); buttocks and hips; trunk (including shoulders); arms and hands.

2. As you exhale, feel the sensations of relaxation occur in the body part on which you are focusing. The sensations to expect are sinking down, slowing down, heaviness, and general relaxation.

3. Once the sensation of relaxation is identified in the body part you are focusing on, or after you have spent two to four breathing cycles on the body part (regardless of whether you have identified the relaxed sensations or not), move your focus of attention to the corresponding body part if there is one (e.g., from right foot to left foot, right lower leg to left lower leg) or to the next body part in sequence (e.g., foot to lower leg, or lower leg to upper leg).

4. Move through the body in sequence until the major body parts have been covered and relaxation has occurred.

5. Remain in the relaxed state until you are ready to end the exercise and come back to an alert state. Then, take a deep breath as you flex, stretch, and open your eyes.

Directions

Assume a comfortable position and, when ready, allow your eyes to close. For several breathing cycles, quietly and passively listen to yourself breathe................

And now, turn your attention to just the exhalation phase of your breathing cycle........and r-e-l-a-x as you exhale........simply permit yourself to l-e-t go............and r-e-l-a-x more and more with each exhalation........................

Now, focus on your right foot and ankle, and as you exhale notice the tension flow out of that foot and ankle........notice that foot and ankle become slightly heavy and more and more r-e-l-a-x-e-d ....As you notice this, allow the foot and ankle to s-i-n-k d-o-w-n and become totally supported by the floor............As you exhale, notice a s-i-n-k-i-n-g d-o-w-n of the foot into the supporting environment...................

And now, ...focus your attention on the left foot and ankle........ and allow it to let go and r-e-l-a-x with your exhalations..........allow that foot and ankle to become slightly h-e-a-v-y,......and more and more relaxed with each exhalation...................

At this time, move your attention to your right lower leg (the calf region)..........As you focus on this area, allow the muscles to r-e-l-a-x...........to l-e-t g-o as you exhale..................simply allow the tensions to flow out of the lower leg as you e-x-h-a-l-e............and r-e-l-a-x...................

Move your attention to the left lower leg and, with each exhalation, feel the muscles of the left lower leg s-i-n-k-i-n-g d-o-w-n......and becoming slightly h-e-a-v-y....................

And now, move your attention to the right thigh.....and feel that part of the body r-e-l-a-x as you exhale...........and r-e-l-a-x as you exhale............

And now, focus your attention on the left thigh. Feel and experience a l-e-t-t-i-n-g g-o with each exhalation.

Focus now on both legs and notice a comfortable heaviness develop with each exhalation as you experience the gentle pull of gravity on the legs.........................

And now, let the relaxation in your legs flow into the buttocks and hips.............As you exhale, allow the muscles to r-e-l-a-x and feel the buttocks s-i-n-k-i-n-g d-o-w-n into the supporting environment as you exhale...................

Now, let this relaxation flow into the trunk area as you exhale and r-e-l-a-x............Feel the trunk sinking down and becoming c-o-m-f-o-r-t-a-b-l-y h-e-a-v-y with each exhalation...........

Focus your attention on the right arm and hand and, as you exhale, allow the relaxation to flow into the right arm and hand. Feel it s-i-n-k-i-n-g d-o-w-n and becoming c-o-m-f-o-r-t-a-b-l-y h-e-a-v-y ....more and more r-e-l-a-x-e-d with each exhalation ....

Now, allow relaxation to move into the left arm............Feel the left arm becoming c-o-m-f-o-r-t-a-b-l-y h-e-a-v-y..........and more and more r-e-l-a-x-e-d with each exhalation.

Now, allow this relaxation to flow into the entire body with each exhalation. Feel, sense and experience a comfortable heaviness........ or a general slowing down of the body............Allow the body now to establish its own pace..........and r-e-l-a-x as you exhale..........and r-e-l-a-x as you exhale.................

Allow this relaxation to occur until you are ready to end the exercise. Then take a deep breath as you flex, stretch, and open your eyes.

Implementation
(See Week One, Chapter 9)

The objective of the first week of the program is to perfect basic relaxation skills and lay the foundation for the upcoming mental training program. To properly lay this base, daily relaxation is required.

Days 1 to 3 focus on the exhalation exercise only. The objective of these early days is to train the body to respond to the exhalation phase of the breathing cycle as the cue to relaxation. The exhalation exercise should be practiced a **minimum** of 3 times daily for 3 to 5 minutes each session.

During days 4 to 7 you will continue to perform the exhalation exercise at least once daily, but, in addition, you will add the sequential relaxation exercise at least twice per day. The sequential exercise requires about 7 to 8 minutes when performed as suggested in the text or when using a cassette tape of the exercise.

On days 6 and 7 of this first week, if you can relax relatively easily, begin to shorten the sequential exercise by grouping body parts together (i.e., instead of the right foot and ankle alone, feel the relaxation in the entire right leg as it becomes heavy, sinks down, and relaxes).

With practice, eventually you will be able to shorten the technique further by grouping the entire lower body together (both right and left legs), the entire trunk of the body (buttocks, hips and trunk), and both arms. The goal of relaxation is to relax and/or calm the body within one to two breaths so the majority of time spent on the program is in the mental conditioning phase.

CHAPTER 6
STEP TWO
POSITIVE AFFIRMATION
STATEMENTS

Once relaxation is mastered, it is time to move on to positive affirmation statements, the next logical step for preparing the mind for mental training. Ideally, positive affirmation statements should be introduced during the second week of the program — after you have perfected the relaxation exercises from the preceeding chapter. If you need to move through the program at an accelerated pace, affirmation statements can be introduced within three to four days of beginning the program since they are easy to incorporate along with your relaxation practice.

What Are
Positive Affirmation Statements?

Positive affirmation statements are short sentences and/or statements which implant in your subconscious mind ideas which are designed to enhance self-image, achieve a positive mental attitude, or help lead you toward a specific goal. They are statements which affirm a belief you want to feed to your subconscious mind. They can be used to counterbalance and overcome the negative thoughts that we so often focus on with our self-talk.

Probably the most quoted positive affirmation is Emile Coue's "Day by day in every way I am getting better and better!" In sporting circles the most well known affirmation is Mohammed Ali's: "I am the greatest!" which he used over and over during his reign as world boxing champion. He repeated this statement so often that not only did he believe it to be true but millions of sports fans around the world believed it to be true as well.

How To Use
Positive Affirmation Statements

Eventually, positive affirmation statements can be used throughout the day as often as possible. For the mental conditioning program, however, you will begin using the statements and repeating them over and over while you are in a relaxed state. When done in a relaxed state, they have a stronger effect on the subconscious mind. In the relaxed state, the rational mind is shut down and accepts the statements without argument.

When using positive affirmation statements, you first perform one of the basic relaxation exercises from Chapter 5 to open the mind up to suggestion. Once in the relaxed state, repeat the positive affirmation statement you have created for yourself five to twenty times in succession. Repeat the statement on the exhalation phase of the breathing cycle. This repetition imprints the thought in the subconscious mind. The affirmations are most effective if you feel the positive emotions that accompany the thoughts.

To be most effective, this process should be repeated two, three or more times daily. I recommend that when beginning the positive affirmation statements you do them every morning upon waking, every evening just before going to sleep, and, if possible, several other times each day. Each time they are done during the first week, do them while in the relaxed state. The more often the statements are repeated, the more rapid and noticeable the desired effect will be.

Developing
Positive Affirmation Statements

The use of affirmation statements for the mental conditioning program requires that the first affirmations be general in nature. At the beginning, you want to prepare your mind for the upcoming visualization. You should not focus on a specific goal other than to open the mind up so you can successfully implement the mental conditioning program. Therefore, statements such as "I can do it," or "I believe I can," or, simply, "I believe," or, for those religious in nature a statement such as "Through the grace of God, I can do it" would be appropriate.

These statements are so general that they are not suggesting in any way what you can do; they are just opening the mind for acceptance as well as for more specific statements to come. In addition, when practicing these statements in the relaxed state, you are practicing concentration as well as relaxation. Do not allow yourself to drift into sleep or your mind to wander when doing the exercise.

GUIDELINES FOR DEVELOPING
AFFIRMATION STATEMENTS

When creating or selecting positive affirmation statements, the following guidelines engender more powerful affirmation.

1. Word the positive affirmation statements so that they are positive in nature. Focus the statement on what you will be doing — not on what you will not be doing. For example, state "I am relaxed" rather than "I am not tense;" or, "I will sink the putt" rather than "I will not miss the putt." Remember, the mind focuses subconsciously on the behavior you are suggesting. If you don't want someone to spill something, you should not state "Don't spill the milk on the rug." This statement focuses on the negative behavior of spilling. The image evoked is spilt milk. Instead, the statement should be reconstructed to reinforce the positive behavior you want carried out. The same idea reworded positively could simply be "Be careful with the milk."

2. Make the positive affirmation statements as brief as possible.

Focus the statements on precisely what you would like to achieve, the exact goal. There is no sense in creating a fog around the goal, disguising it with unnecessary words.

3. Select vivid words for your positive affirmation statements. The way you state or verbalize something can influence your mood and feelings, so be precise as well as vivid in selecting the statement. Each time you repeat the affirmation, you want to reinforce the emotional feeling that accompanies the action it describes.

4. Use the present tense whenever possible in your positive affirmation statements. This makes the visualization as well as the emotions evoked more vivid and more believable.

Read the sample affirmation statements that follow, then use these guidelines, and on page 80, develop at least three positive affirmation statements for use in your personal program.

Sample Affirmation Statements

Not only can affirmation statements be used to prepare the mind for imagery when you first begin the mental conditioning program, but they also can be used throughout the program for all areas of your life. The following list of sample affirmation statements is not limited to the sporting field. They have been developed according to the guidelines discussed previously. These statements can be used as examples to follow when developing your own. However, to achieve the best results, I suggest that you create your own affirmation statements to meet your particular needs.

STATEMENTS TO ENHANCE SELF-IMAGE AND ACHIEVE A POSITIVE MENTAL ATTITUDE

"Every day in every way, I am better and better."
"I am filled with loving kindness."
"I am at peace with nature — and myself."
"I am happy and content with my job."
"I am a success."
"Optimism makes me enthusiastic."

STATEMENTS TO ALLEVIATE WORRY

"I live for the present."
"This is a great day."
"Problems are just opportunities in disguise."

STATEMENTS TO FOSTER RELAXATION, HEALTH, AND HEALING

"I am relaxed."
"I am healthy, happy, and relaxed."
"My body heals itself."
"Pain free, happy me!"
"I am healthy, refreshed, and full of energy."
"I believe."
"I forgive others."
"I am in God's healing hands."
"The doctor dresses the wound, God heals it."

STATEMENTS TO ENCOURAGE WEIGHT LOSS

"I am proud of my ideal weight." (Visualize how you look at this weight.)
"I feel pride and joy as I approach my desired weight."
"Every day in every way, I am thinner and thinner."
"I am satisfied; my hunger has been eliminated."
"I desire carrots."

Implementation

(See Week Two, Chapter 9)

Once relaxation is perfected, it is time to incorporate positive affirmation statements with the relaxation. Although affirmations can be incorporated within three to four days of beginning the program, ideally you should wait until the second week. This will give you adequate time to learn the relaxation exercises in Chapter 5, both of which must be perfected for the variations discussed in Chapter 10.

While in a relaxed state (using one of the exercises from Chapter 5), repeat the positive affirmation statement you have created for yourself five to twenty times. Repeat the statement on the exhalation phase of the breathing cycle. This should be done at least three times per day. Use the same general affirmation for the entire week (week number two of the program outlined in Chapter 9).

After one week of using general affirmation statements you can create additional statements that are more specific in nature. At least one time daily use a general statement. At other practice sessions you can use a more specific statement geared toward a specific goal. Use affirmation statements throughout the program using general statements and specific statements in alternating sessions.

As you move through the mental conditioning program and feel comfortable with each of the four steps, you should then begin using affirmation statements throughout the day, not just at times when you are in a relaxed state. Use the statements during the course of your daily activities such as when walking, going between appointments, and while working out. Initially you will get the greatest benefit while in a relaxed state because the statements will help prepare the mind for the upcoming steps, but, eventually, you will derive as much benefit from affirmations while doing them in an alert state.

CHAPTER 7
STEP THREE
MENTAL RECALL

Relaxation puts the body in the proper state for mental conditioning by lowering the arousal level and slowing and/or shutting down the rational mind. Positive affirmation statements open the mind for mental conditioning by laying a base of positive beliefs so that the mind will be receptive for the upcoming mental practice. Mental recall is then introduced as the third step of the mental conditioning program. Mental recall is important in the overall program because it reaffirms the positive nature of the program by "reliving" or "replaying" past situations in which you have been successful.

When "recalling" these past experiences, you should use as many "senses" as possible (i.e., sight, feel (kinesthetic), smell, etc.). The more detail one can recall the more effective the recall experience will be. Therefore, it is important to include as many details as you can remember of the actual situation you are recalling.

Suggestions for Successful Mental Recall

I suggest the following guidelines for successful mental recall practice.

SELECT A RECALL EXPERIENCE OR EXPERIENCES IN WHICH YOU PERFORMED PERFECTLY OR NEAR PERFECTLY

Mental recall reinforces a previous positive experience and imprints that experience in your mind. Obviously then, you want to select an experience or experiences in which you performed at your best; one in which you put everything together, both physically and mentally, and/or one in which you accomplished a sought after goal or came through when the chips were down.

Keep in mind that the event selected for mental recall does not have to be one that was entirely successful, but you can use a portion of an experience that was highly successful.

Example One

You might select a specific putt you sank from 50 feet. Maybe the entire round of golf was not satisfactory, but the putt was one of your best shots ever — the one part of the round that stands out.

In this example, remember how you felt before the putt as you lined it up, what you were thinking about prior to the putt, how relaxed and confident you were, etc. Then feel the movement as you stroked the ball and actually visualize the path of the ball as it rolls across the green and into the hole. But don't stop there. Mental practice has a greater effect on the subconscious mind when the instructions are emotionalized. So, feel the excitement and elation of having dropped the putt. Then you may move to a different golf game to recall another shot.

Example Two

In a basketball game recall a free throw you sank with 2 seconds to go that tied the game and sent it into overtime. If your team did not win the game, your recall should emphasize those parts of the game that were picture perfect — when you were at your best. Each shot or pass that you select for recall can be an entire recall event in and of itself or it can be part of a recall event.

In selecting recall events, whenever possible, focus on your best effort to date or several parts of a good performance. If you defeated last year's conference champion, recall as much as you can — but only the positive portions of it. If you came from behind to win, focus only on your comeback or positive parts of it.

While coaching football at a small college our team fell behind 28-0 and was stopped at the two yard line as time expired in the first half. This game stands out because the team did not feel defeated; in fact, the opposite was true. At halftime, the mood of the entire team and coaches was a positive one. In the second half we played error free and came back to win 35-28. The feeling of positive expectancy — knowing you can win — could be used in this recall event. The positive feelings of the first half and halftime could be used as well as the positive effort during the second half, disregarding the poor playing of the first half.

RECALL THE EXPERIENCE IN AS MUCH DETAIL AS POSSIBLE

After you have identified a recall event, and before you begin practicing, make a written list of as much detail as you can recall consciously (see Figure 7-1): your feelings before the event; your confidence; the actual event as seen from your own eyes; the excitement, elation, energy, etc. Following the event visualize your friends, teammates, coach, (if these apply) and picture yourself being congratulated, receiving an award or trophy, etc.

The key to developing detail is to use as many senses as possible. Use sight — what you saw from your own eyes as if you are actually experiencing the event again; use smell — if outdoors, was there the smell of trees, the grass, hay? If indoors, could you smell sweat, the room? Use feel — what was the temperature? Was there heat from the sun? Were you cool from the wind? Use kinesthetic feel — what did it feel like as you performed the skill? Use sound — was there crowd noise, or was there silence? Use taste — did you taste sweat as it ran into your mouth? Did you taste chalk if you are a gymnast? Use emotions — how did it feel when you were successful? Emotionalizing makes it vivid for the nervous system and adds to the success of the recall.

FIGURE 7-1

MENTAL RECALL WORKSHEET

DESCRIBE THE EVENT YOU WILL BE RECALLING

EXPERIENCES AND SENSATIONS FELT PRIOR TO THE EVENT
Emotional Feelings
Level of Confidence
Energy/Stress Levels
Temperature
Smell
Sound
Thoughts/Expectations/Goal
Others

ACTUAL PERFORMANCE (WHAT YOU EXPERIENCED AT VARIOUS STAGES OF THE PERFORMANCE)

Emotional Feelings
Smell
Sound
Kinesthetic Feelings
Taste
Temperature
Confidence
What You Saw from Your Own Eyes
Others

COMPLETION OF EVENT

Emotional Feelings
Thoughts
Level of Confidence
Level of Stress
What You Saw
Other Things You Experienced

ADDITIONAL COMMENTS/OBSERVATIONS ABOUT THE RECALL EXPERIENCE

After you have written the key details to recall, review the list prior to doing the recall in the relaxed state. When you perform the recall event in the relaxed state, you'll probably recall more sensations than those you've written down. Immediately after the recall add the new sensations to the written list for future practice sessions.

RELIVE THE EXPERIENCE FROM INSIDE THE BODY — JUST AS IT ACTUALLY HAPPENED

The mental recall, as well as the upcoming mental rehearsal, should be lived from "your own mind's eye." See the experience just as if you are doing it yourself — from within your own body. As Chevreul's pendulum illustrated in Chapter 2, if you visualize the movement from within, you lay a blueprint in the nervous system as well as the skeletal system of how to perform the skill. So, you want to visualize from within and "feel" the proper kinesthetic movements. As you do this, you are actually practicing the proper skills and laying the blueprint for future successes.

If you have difficulty imagining the recall from within, you may want to watch yourself from a distance or see yourself on a screen. Many athletes who are used to viewing films, television, or video tapes of their own or others' performances initially can see the performance better from a distance, from outside their body.

If this is the case, begin by watching yourself perform as if you are performing on a screen. Visualize how you felt and how you moved. See your grace, confidence, agility, strength, and aggressiveness as you moved. First, watch them from a distance; then move inside your body and "feel" these same characteristics from within your body as you perform the skills from your own mind's eye.

The goal is to perform from within your own body to achieve maximum benefits. So, if you need to start by viewing yourself from a distance, move within your body as soon as possible.

USE PROPER SPEED

To best feel the kinesthetic sense of actually performing a skill, it is imperative that you relive the experience at the proper speed. If you go to slow motion, not only does the feel of the movement disappear, but the other senses are often distorted or removed from the recall (e.g., the sounds get distorted).

Slow motion can be used occasionally to analyze a movement and to make a correction when a movement is improper. However, once the proper movement sequence is correct, do all of your practice of both recall and rehearsal events at the proper speed.

CARRY EACH RECALL EXPERIENCE
THROUGH TO COMPLETION

It is important that each recall experience be a complete experience in and of itself. How you carry a recall experience through to completion will vary from sport to sport. Some sports will be "fast moving" and the recall practiced may be the entire skill while other sports could be classified as "slow moving" and the recall may focus on various parts of the skill.

Recall for Fast Moving Sports

A fast moving sport is one in which the entire event or skill you are practicing takes place over a short period of time. Examples of fast moving sports are putting the shot, a jump for a pole vaulter, a pass or a kick in soccer, several volleys in tennis or racquetball, a swing in golf or a shot or pass in basketball. In sports that are fast moving, you can visualize the entire experience and "see" the end result such as the shot landing at the 54 foot mark, the golf ball landing near the cup, the basketball swishing through the hoop, etc. As you perform this type of recall take the experience through to completion and feel the elation you felt when the end result happened. When doing this type of recall, you may want to repeat the recall event numerous times during a session or you may want to select several different recall experiences.

Recall for Slow Moving Sports

If the event you are working to improve is a slow moving sport one which takes several minutes or several hours to complete, you can focus on key aspects of the event for the recall experience. Examples of slow moving sports are a 10 K run, a marathon, a triathalon, a distance event in swimming, biking, etc.

Using a distance run as an example, you may focus first on how you felt before the race — your tension level, feelings of confidence, etc. Then focus on the start as you move to establish position in the race; then move ahead to key phases during the race such as a long hill — feeling the strength, confidence and the rhythm you felt as you were running that hill; then you may move to the last 1/2 or 1/4 mile, recalling your exhaustion, the heaviness of the legs (be realistic), yet the mental toughness you displayed as you challenged the person in front of you and passed that runner and pushed yourself through the finish line. Then recall the feelings of exhaustion and exhilaration you felt as you realized you accomplished your goal. Once again, be sure to emotionalize the experience. Take it through to completion by recalling the feelings as you were congratulated by opponents, your coach and friends, and how you felt as you saw your name, time and place on the results sheet, how you felt while getting an award for your performance.

So, in a slow moving event, the entire event does not have to be practiced to receive maximum benefits. As long as you practice key parts of an experience, the mental recall will be successful in preparing you for the fourth and final step of the mental conditioning program.

REHEARSE DAILY

The key to mental conditioning is the same as it is for physical conditioning and skill acquisition — **Regular Practice!** A serious athlete would never consider practicing or working out on an occasional basis. To acquire and refine a skill, regular practice is a prerequisite. Yet, so often, I hear athletes say "I practice mentally whenever I need to." Undoubtedly, these athletes are not as highly motivated as they could be since they are honing the physical side of the ax and not the mental side. They are leaving part of their performance to chance, which is risky indeed.

Mental practice, as with physical practice has to be done on a daily or near-daily basis if you are to derive maximum benefits from it. Mental preparation is a skill, and like any skill, regular practice allows it to become a positive habit.

STAY ALERT

As mentioned several times before, it is important that you remain alert as you go through mental practice. One of the side benefits of relaxation is an improvement in concentration if you can train yourself to remain alert while deeply relaxed. It's easy to have the mind wander during both mental recall and mental rehearsal. When performing recall or rehearsal, remember, to be most effective, you want to be as vivid as possible with your visualizations. Obviously, you will not be vivid if your mind is wandering or you are falling asleep.

If you find you have difficulty remaining alert when doing the recall or rehearsal, here are some things you can try.

1. Shorten the practice session. Imagery is most effective when done in small amounts. Most sessions of imagery should be concluded within 5 to 8 minutes from the beginning of the relaxation. If you practice for longer periods of time, the law of diminishing returns takes over. Therefore, adjust the time frame to your level of alertness during the techniques.

2. Break up the practice session. If you find your mind is beginning to wander, come out of the relaxed state by flexing, stretching, opening the eyes and taking a deep breath. Once you are alert, go back to where you left off in the recall session and continue the exercise.

3. Don't get too deeply relaxed. Generally, you do not have to be as deeply relaxed for mental recall since you have already accomplished the event you are recalling. However, if, you have difficulty doing the recall because the rational mind will not accept the recall event, you may have to practice for several days in a deep state of relaxation. This is most likely to happen if you are in a slump or if the recall event was a one time occurance that you've not come close to again.

Implementation

(See Week Three, Chapter 9)

Use the following sequence when first introducing mental recall.

1. Relax. Using one of the techniques presented in Chapter 5, go into a relaxed state. Get as deeply relaxed as needed without losing your alertness. If you are calm, relaxed and still alert, proceed directly to positive affirmation statements. If you are too relaxed and, therefore, not alert, come out of the relaxed state, relax for 1 or 2 breathing cycles, and proceed to the next step.

2. Positive Affirmation Statements. For 2 to 5 breaths, repeat your affirmation statements on each exhalation. When repeated on the exhalation phase of the breathing cycle, you may become more relaxed during this phase. But again, remember, do not get too relaxed. If you find you are getting too relaxed at this point, spend less time on the relaxation, less time on the affirmation statements, and/or come out of the relaxed state before you proceed. If you are relaxed or calm and still alert, proceed directly to mental recall without coming out of that state.

3. Mental Recall. Perform the recall event or events that you have listed and described as in Figure 7-1. Recall the event with as much detail as possible, using as many senses as possible, taking the event or events through to completion. Enjoy the feelings you felt when you accomplished your goal during the recall.

4. When completed, flex, stretch, take a deep breath, and open your eyes. After coming out of the technique the first few times you perform these three steps together, analyze the recall and add any sensations, feelings, thoughts, that came to mind to your list.

CHAPTER 8
STEP FOUR
MENTAL REHEARSAL

The fourth and final step in the mental conditioning program is mental rehearsal. The previous three steps established the foundation of the program. Relaxation placed your body in the relaxed state to prepare or open the mind for mental conditioning. Positive affirmation statements affirm a belief you want to feed to your subconscious mind. Mental recall provides the strength for the upcoming program by recalling, step by step, feelings of success by implanting in your subconscious images and feelings of success you've already experienced.

Now, through mental rehearsal, you will complete the program by using the powers of your mind to improve future performances.

What Is Mental Rehearsal?

Mental rehearsal is a skill, a process during which you use your mind to visualize desired results of a future event. The key is to remember that during mental rehearsal **you will guide the mind — be in control of it — to accomplish desired results.**

You've used visualization before. We all have. But all too often visualization is used in a negative, destructive manner. People use the detrimental side of visualization by viewing undesired results as well as by worrying, thus imprinting in the subconscious mind negative thoughts, feelings and behaviors that erode self-concept and reinforce negative behaviors.

Using the above definition of mental rehearsal, we will be focusing on the positive — selected goals and behaviors that you would like to achieve rather than the negative thoughts and worries that so often fill one's mind. In this way we will be etching a blueprint of these desired results into our subconscious.

Why Use Mental Rehearsal?

Mental rehearsal is used in the mental conditioning program:

1. To enhance self-image. You always perform consistently with your self-image. If you are not performing up to the level of your abilities, it is quite probable that your self-image is not at the level it should be. By repeatedly visualizing positive upcoming events, you can strengthen the self-image base which was laid by mental recall.

2. To practice future events. Mental rehearsal can be used to practice future events which are likely to happen. You can not only visualize in your mind what you want to happen, but you can also visualize every conceivable situation that could happen. This would be done to help you prepare for and respond to each of these possible situations.

When working with cross country runners in preparing for major meets, I have the runners visualize the race in all types of weather. They picture themselves running confidently, relaxed and strong in cold weather, wet weather, sunny

*weather, snowy weather. They also know that
inclement weather often "psyches out" their
opponents while it has no effect on them.
Recently, after working on these images for a
week prior to the national meet, the runners
finished second in the nation. They came closer
to the national championship than at any time
in the history of the school while running the
meet in almost a foot of snow on a cold, windy
day.*

3. To visualize performances that supplement physical training
with neuromuscular practice. As illustrated with Chevreul's
pendulum, visualizing a movement causes the body to respond
subliminally. Research points out that, if repeated regularly, the proper
neuromuscular blueprint (i.e., the proper sequence for the nervous
system and muscular system to react) is established to enhance and
reinforce motor skills (movement).

Goals And Mental Rehearsal

To be successful with visualization you must have clear and
concise pictures of the desired behavior. The success mechanism in
our body is activated by goals. Research indicates that successful
people (1) all have Goals — they know exactly what they want, and
(2) resolve to pay the price necessary to accomplish these goals.
Obviously, one cannot resolve to pay the price, in fact, one can't know
what the price is, unless one has identified the goals in the first place.

To be successful, one must not only define goals but also have a
general understanding of goals and of how to use them properly.
Although an entire book could be written on goals, our purpose here
is to identify several key concepts regarding goals that make visualization more successful.

GOALS PROVIDE DIRECTION

There is an old saying in education that states "If you don't know where you're going, you're liable to end up somewhere else." This is true in all aspects of our life. You don't receive a college diploma because you happen to be walking by an auditorium on commencement day. To accomplish that degree, you had to have a goal. You knew what you wanted, knew what you would have to pay to accomplish the goal, and put years of effort into taking classes, studying, and working in a specific direction — to get the degree.

The goal provided direction. When you know what your goal is, you know when you get off track and can take corrective action to get going in the right direction again. Without goals, you can't assess whether you are on track and moving in the right direction or not.

Goals vary from person to person. One athlete may have a goal of making the cut, another's goal may be to be a starter, while yet another's may be to make the All-Conference or All-State team. Once you have a goal, you have direction. You can then determine what you're willing to do to accomplish that goal; and you also have a measuring stick to see if you're on course.

GOALS SHOULD BE SPECIFIC

To be most successful using visualization, you should develop specific goals. If mental rehearsal is to complement your physical training, you need to establish exactly what you want.

The top five runners of a cross country team I once worked with had already qualified for the conference and national meets. The two spots still open for the team for these two meets were to be filled based on the results of an upcoming race in which the top five runners would not run. In preparation for this meet the remaining runners, with input from their coach, identified individual goals. Their competition was ranked in the top five teams in the nation. The coach as well as the team members assumed they would be running against the opposition minus their top 5 to 7 runners. Goals were selected based on this assumption.

During mental preparation, each runner identified a specific goal — a place he wanted to finish, a time he wanted to run, an individual he wanted to beat, or a combination of the above. The team goal was to beat the second team of the opposition — a goal that could be accomplished if they all ran well and achieved their individual goals.

For the week preceding the race, the members of the squad used positive affirmation statements and visualized their specific goals, including receiving their place numbers as they came through the finishing chute at the conclusion of the race.

To the team's surprise as well as the coach's, the opposition came to the meet with their first team not the second as expected. In spite of this, they not only beat their opponent, but they came close to accomplishing their individual goals as well.

When questioned following the meet, the runners indicated two items of interest: (1) they practiced their goals so often and believed them to such an extent, that even knowing they were running against the better group, they believed they could achieve their specific goals; and (2) they would have selected "lesser" goals had they known in advance they were facing the first team. This story not only indicates the importance of identifying specific goals, but it also leads to the next point.

GOALS SHOULD BE HIGH BUT ACHIEVABLE

You should select goals within your reach yet high enough to allow you to move to the next plateau of achievement.

When working with athletes I often tell them to select a goal that is slightly out of their reach. It's amazing to see how often these "out of reach" goals are accomplished. But remember, the goal should be realistic as well. Shooting a hole in one in golf on every hole would be nice, but it's not realistic. In sum, goals should be a challenge but still be within reach.

GOALS SHOULD BE WRITTEN

If goals are to be specific and provide direction, they must be written down. Many people argue that they have thought about their goals and know what they are and, therefore, don't need to write them down. However, I have found that unwritten goals often remain vague. Committing goals to paper helps you make them more specific. You gain a new perspective when they are in this more concrete form. Once goals are in written form you can add sub-goals as well as analyze, change and update the goals on a regular basis.

The key to success is to identify the most important goals and then regularly visualize the achievement of these goals. Establish a major goal and related sub-goals; then use the mental conditioning program to accomplish these goals. Often athletes change goals on a regular basis. This constant vacillation prevents success rather than helps it.

At this time you should do the following exercise to identify and analyze your goals. Then you will have a specific, written goal to work toward for the mental rehearsal portion of the mental conditioning program.

Writing Your Goal

Using the guidelines discussed above, write 4 or 5 goals that you would like to accomplish for your sport.

A.

B.

C.

D.

E.

Examine each of the goals and rank them in order of importance in the space before the letter. For example, rank the most important goal 1, second most important 2, etc.

Once you have identified the most important goal, the one which the other goals may fall under, rewrite the goal in the space below. Be sure the goal is specific; high, but achievable; and provides direction.

Goal:

Guidelines For
Practicing Mental Rehearsal

Once you have selected a specific goal, it is time to add mental rehearsal to the mental conditioning program. The guidelines for mental rehearsal are similiar to those for mental recall.

1. Visualize a performance that is near perfect, positive, and during which **you accomplish your goal.**

2. Visualize the experience in detail, using as many senses as possible.

3. Visualize the performance from inside the body as if **you** are actually performing.

4. Use proper speed.

5. Carry the visualization through to completion.

6. Rehearse regularly. I suggest at least two to three rehearsal practice sessions per day. This is especially important as you near the competition.

7. Stay alert

Implementation
(See Week Four, Chapter 9)

It is now time to incorporate all four steps of the mental conditioning program. Before you add step four to the program, a specific goal should be identified. If you have not already done so go back to the section titled "Goals Should Be Written" and complete that section to identify the most important goal. **Be sure you write down the goal.** This helps you identify an exact, rather than a vague, goal.

Now, perform a short relaxation technique, repeat 2 to 5 positive affirmation statements, and do a brief recall event. If you are getting too relaxed at this time, take a deep breath and come out of the relaxed state. If you are still alert, but calm, proceed directly to the mental rehearsal. If you came out of the relaxed state, relax for one or two breathing cycles until you are calm; then perform the mental rehearsal, using the guidelines discussed in this chapter.

Before doing an actual rehearsal, read the example in Appendix A which incorporates the guidelines into an actual practice session.

"I never hit a shot, not even in practice, without having a very sharp, in-focus picture of it in my head."

JACK NICKLAUS
Golfer

PART III
STRATEGIES FOR SUCCESS

P art I laid the base for the use of mental conditioning in athletics. Part II covered the four steps of the Mental Conditioning Program. Knowing what has to be done is one thing — doing it is another. Part III of *The Mindset for Winning* clarifies the actual implementation of the program. This section includes suggestions for accomplishing success.

Chapter 9 pulls together the four steps of the Mental Conditioning Program and leads you through a week-to-week outline with suggestions on how to accomplish each week's objectives. I also propose ideas for implementing a condensed program, because time restrictions often force one away from the ideal.

Chapter 10, "Beyond the Basics" discusses additional uses for the skills described in this book. It includes suggestions and/or techniques for: utilizing relaxation when needed during an actual competition; improving concentration and regaining concentration during a sporting event; performing mental rehearsal during the actual competition; and using imagery in the healing process.

CHAPTER 9
IMPLEMENTING THE PROGRAM

To be successful with mental conditioning, it is important to establish a daily practice schedule. The term "training" or "conditioning" (i.e., "mental training" or "mental conditioning") literally means "regular practice." Physical practice is more effective when done on a daily basis than when done once or twice a week. The same holds true for mental practice. The more often it is done, the more effective the results will be.

Suggestions For Success

KEEP THE PROGRAM SIMPLE
There are many different mental training or peak performance programs available today. Most of them are excellent. However, in trying to cover all the bases, these programs have become so complicated and time consuming that they often are not practical to implement. In working with athletes over the years, I've found that most, from weekend golfers to professionals, have a limited amount of additional time to devote to their sport. As such, I've found that an

easy program with minimal time requirements is more likely to be followed on a day-to-day basis.

ESTABLISH A DAILY GOAL FOR IMPLEMENTATION

An established daily goal is a prerequisite for success. This daily goal is not your mental conditioning goal but your goal for implementing the program — what you will do each day to be successful. A sample daily goal would be to practice once a day for week one; or better yet, to practice twice or three times daily. Without a clear implementation goal your chances for success are diminished. Remember the key points about goals was discussed in Chapter 8. Then, establish your daily goal for implementing the program and write it out (state the minimum) under the Daily Goal heading for each week in the Four Week Success Program that follows.

ESTABLISH A REGULAR PRACTICE SCHEDULE

Establish a daily time for your mental training. It is best to link your scheduled practice with some regularly occurring daily event, e.g., before getting out of bed in the morning; before falling asleep at night; during a coffee break; before or after a workout. Or, include your practice on your daily "To Do" list as you schedule each day. Keep in mind — if mental training is not a priority, it won't get done on a regular basis. Therefore, make it a priority!

LOG EACH PRACTICE SESSION

If you really want to change behavior, keeping a written log or diary is the best way to improve your chances for success. Charting, recording, and evaluating your practice sessions as well as your progress has been found to be an excellent motivational tool. This also is an excellent way to chart the progress you are making toward your achievement goals.

These daily logs or diaries improve your experiences and your chances for success because they serve as a reminder. They keep your mind on your goals on a daily basis. Daily implementation logs appear in *The Mindset for Winning Log Book* as well as *The Mindset for Winning Workbook*, both available from the publisher.

A Four-Week Success Program

Write the major goal you want to accomplish below.

MAJOR GOAL (SEE PAGE 71)

WEEK 1 OBJECTIVE:
TO LEARN AND PERFECT BASIC RELAXATION

Daily Goal

Three practice sessions per day — 3 to 5 minutes each session.

Days 1-3

Practice the exhalation exercise at least three times daily for 3 to 5 minutes each session.

Days 4-7

Practice the exhalation exercise at least one time daily and the sequential relaxation exercise at least two times daily.

Comments

As you near the end of the week you will find that it takes less and less time to get into a relaxed or calm state. When this occurs you will be spending more time in the relaxed state for each practice session. This is helpful because the benefits derived from relaxation are from the time spent in the relaxed state. In addition, you will want to train the body to get in the relaxed state more quickly so the bulk of time for mental conditioning eventually will be spent on mental recall or mental rehearsal.

WEEK 2 OBJECTIVE:
TO LAY THE FOUNDATION FOR THE UPCOMING
MENTAL RECALL AND REHEARSAL

Daily Goal

At least 3 daily practice sessions incorporating both relaxation and positive affirmation statements.

Information Needed

You will need the positive affirmation statements prior to beginning this week's program. In the space below, write and refine 3 affirmation statements based on the guidelines discussed on pages 51 to 52. Select the best general statement and use it for days 1 to 3.

Positive Affirmation Statements:

1.

2.

3.

Days 1-3

Relax, using one of the exercises from week 1. While in the relaxed state, repeat the positive affirmation statement that you identified as best 5 to 20 times. Repeat the statement in your mind on each exhalation. **Caution** — do not fall asleep or allow your mind to drift during these practice sessions (although you can drift into sleep after the session if you so desire). If you are in danger of sleep, shorten the practice session or come out of the relaxed state for a moment and then go back into the relaxed state and complete the exercise. Remember — if you are to derive the benefit of improved concentration, you must concentrate throughout the entire practice session.

Days 4-7

Relax, then repeat one or more of the remaining affirmation statements during each session.

Comments

Remember that the goal of week 2 is to lay the foundation for the upcoming imagery. You can stay with one affirmation or use several during each session after week two. In addition, you can and should start repeating affirmation statements while doing other daily activities. Repeat them while working out, or walking, or at other convenient times. You do not need to be in the relaxed state to derive benefit from affirmations, but you should continue to do them with relaxation as a preliminary activity before doing the upcoming mental imagery.

WEEK 3 OBJECTIVE:
TO INTRODUCE MENTAL RECALL AND FURTHER
PREPARE THE MIND FOR MENTAL REHEARSAL

Daily Goal

Two to three practice sessions daily as well as repeating affirmation statements during other activities daily.

Information Needed

For week 3 you need to select one or more recall events. Select the recall event and review it prior to each practice session. Selecting and developing recall events was discussed previously (see Figure 7-1). In the space below list 1 to 3 recall events or parts of events that you will use for this week's practice sessions.

Recall Events

1.

2.

3.

Days 1-3

For each practice session perform basic relaxation followed by 2 to 5 positive affirmation statements on each exhalation. While in the calm or relaxed state, yet still alert, relive the recall experience from inside the body — just as it actually happened. Be sure to recall the event in as much detail as possible while using as many senses as possible. See pages 55 to 62 to review basic points regarding successful mental recall. For days 1 to 3 use the same recall event for each practice session.

Days 4-7

Use the same procedure as for days 1 to 3, but you can alter or replace the mental recall event with other events or parts of other events.

WEEK 4 OBJECTIVE:
TO INCORPORATE MENTAL REHEARSAL TO PRACTICE FOR AN UPCOMING EVENT

Daily Goal

Three sessions per day incorporating relaxation, positive affirmation statements, mental recall, and mental rehearsal into the daily routine.

Days 1-3

Relax (briefly so as not to get too relaxed), do 2 to 5 positive affirmation statements, and do a brief recall event. Then, come out of the relaxed state for 5 to 20 seconds by stretching and taking a deep breath. At this time, relax for one or two breathing cycles (relaxation should happen quickly if you have followed the routine outlined for weeks 1 to 3). Then perform the mental rehearsal in detail, incorporating as many sensations and feelings as you can. Review pages 71 and 72 for more information regarding mental rehearsal.

Days 4-7

Using the same sequence outlined in days 1 to 3 above, use mental rehearsal to practice short-term goals as well as long-term goals. You may combine long-term and short-term goals for the same session or you can practice one goal at one session and different goals at another session. Be sure to spend daily sessions on your main goals. For example, if your main goal for the year is to win a specific tournament, be sure you practice that goal daily. Sub-goals, such as winning the current week's meet or competition, may be practiced for 3 to 7 days prior to that actual competition. These sub-goals may change from week to week, and you may want to spend 1 or 2 sessions daily on these. But do not neglect your main goals!

A Condensed Program

The program outlined above is an ideal approach to achieve the maximum benefit from mental training. Yet, you may be introduced to this program at a time when you do not have 4 or 5 weeks to lay the proper foundation. You may want to achieve benefits from imagery but only have days or a week or two to implement the program for an upcoming event. If this is the case the program will need to be adapted to meet your situation. When adapting the program to a shorter time frame, there are several key points to keep in mind.

SHORTEN THE TIME SPENT ON RELAXATION

Spending 1 to 3 days on the relaxation phase may be sufficient if you practice 3 to 5 times per day or if you already have relatively good skills at basic relaxation. If the relaxation is shortened, do the exhalation exercise only. However, keep in mind that the benefits derived from relaxation as outlined in Chapter 4 may not be fully achieved in this condensed program.

COMBINE RELAXATION WITH POSITIVE AFFIRMATION STATEMENTS

Steps one and two, relaxation and positive affirmation statements, can be combined and learned at the same time. Once again, you would have to decide how much time you have to lay the foundation for the imagery. In some situations we have successfully combined relaxation, positive affirmation statements, and mental recall from the beginning of the program.

PRACTICE MORE OFTEN

The shorter the time span you have to lay the foundation, the more time you should devote to daily practice sessions. Rather than practice 2 to 3 times daily for 3 to 5 minutes each, practice 4 to 6 times daily for 3 to 5 minutes each. Remember, do not lengthen the time of each session. Rather, increase the number of sessions done per day. Research points out that 7 to 8 minutes seems to be the maximum time per session to achieve desired results. When the practice sessions get longer, the law of diminishing returns comes into play.

ADAPT THE PROGRAM TO FIT YOUR NEEDS

If you are in a slump and your self-confidence has been eroded, put your major effort into mental recall. If you feel confident, put the bulk of your time into mental rehearsal. It is important to analyze your situation and then adapt the program to fit your needs.

CHAPTER 10
BEYOND THE BASICS

As we learn more and more about the mind/body connection, self-image and mental imagery, we begin to realize that the information can be applied differently to various situations. This chapter shows you how you can adapt and use the key concepts to improve your chances for success.

Relaxation During Competition

A characteristic of peak performers in all walks of life is their ability to control their bodies — including their ability to relax in highly stressful situations. This ability can be developed in several ways. Research has found that people who perform relaxation techniques on a regular basis are in greater control of their body's reaction to stressful situations, both physiologically and psychologically. Therefore, regular relaxation in a non-stressful environment contributes to controlling stress when you are in a stressful situation.

It is also possible to control stress by performing relaxation techniques while you are actually under stress. Since basic relaxation has already been discussed in Chapter 5, this section will introduce

Instant Relaxation techniques that can be used when needed during actual competition.

INSTANT RELAXATION

The term Instant Relaxation (IR) represents a group of techniques that can yield results within one to four breathing cycles or 5 to 20 seconds. These techniques are both short and easy to do. If you have perfected basic relaxation then you have the key to learning these IR techniques. Although this is not a requirement for success, I suggest you spend at least one week practicing the exhalation exercise before practicing the techniques presented here. The exhalation exercise, as well as the sequential technique, trains you to use the breathing cycle as your cue to relaxing the body. Once your body is trained to react to the breathing cycle as the cue for relaxation in the non-stressful environment, you should practice the Instant Relaxation techniques during practice sessions for your sport. When you can relax using the IR techniques in practice, you are ready to apply them to actual competition.

Advantages of IR Techniques

Although Instant Relaxation techniques do not take the place of deep muscle relaxation, they do offer many advantages not found in the deep muscle techniques and thus complement basic relaxation skills.

1. IR techniques can be done anywhere. You don't need to close your eyes, have quiet surroundings, or mentally withdraw from the environment. This is especially useful during athletic contests. IR techniques can be used any time you feel relaxation or stress control is needed as you prepare for a free throw, line up a putt, or get ready to serve or return the gamepoint in tennis.

2. IR techniques are quick and easy to do. They can be done anytime you have 5 to 20 seconds available.

3. IR techniques can help conserve energy, reduce unwanted muscle tension, and cut down on fatigue. This can be especially helpful to the athlete prior to and during an athletic contest. They can be used during timeouts, between heats, and, depending on the

sport, during any lull in the competition. The football player can use them between plays and still remain mentally alert, the baseball player between pitches or innings, and the golfer while walking between shots. If done during actual competition, you have the advantage of conserving energy that may be needed later on in the competition, and you will remain relaxed, yet alert — the state in which you perform best physically while maintaining your ability to concentrate.

Sample IR Techniques

THE BRIEF BODY SCAN TECHNIQUE

The Brief Body Scan is a variation of the Sequential Relaxation Technique presented in Chapter 5. It is the easiest IR technique to learn because it requires just four breaths to do. However, because it is the longest IR technique, it may not be as useful as the Deep Breath Technique which follows. Since it is the easiest to learn, it should be learned first.

Description

With a total of four normal breaths, body parts are relaxed sequentially within 20 to 30 seconds (this time requirement limits its use in some sports).

Take a deep breath, and, as you exhale from the first breath, allow your jaw to relax, let go, and become heavy. Take a normal breath, and, as you exhale, allow your shoulders to relax. As you exhale from the third breath, allow your arms and hands to relax. And, as you exhale from the fourth breath, allow your legs to relax.

THE DEEP BREATH TECHNIQUE

Because the Deep Breath is a one-breath technique it is the fastest and probably the most useful to use during actual competition. In fact, many athletes use this technique without even realizing it. If practiced regularly, the body is trained to respond to the one breath so that you can relax and control arousal level whenever you need to do so.

Description

Take a deep breath and hold it for a count of one to five seconds. As you exhale, feel the body slowing down, letting go of tension, and relaxing.

With practice, you will be able to take a deep breath and immediately exhale away tensions. If your sport requires that you become invigorated, then you should feel the body letting go of tension, relaxing and becoming energetic as you exhale.

Concentration

Regardless of whether you are attempting to improve your ability to drop a putt on a quiet golf course, sink a free throw while hundreds of fans try to distract you, or hit a 90 mph fastball, the ability to concentrate, is a prerequisite to consistently high performance. However, as important as concentration is, very few athletes understand what it is. This creates a problem because if you don't understand what concentration is, how do you improve it?

WHAT IS CONCENTRATION

First of all, concentration is a mental skill that like all other skills, can be perfected with practice. In sporting circles, concentration would best be defined as a narrowing or focusing of one's attention on a specific subject (task) to the exclusion of other subjects. Concentration can also be defined as a relaxed state of being mentally alert.

Many athletes have the misconception that telling oneself to concentrate is the way to improve concentration. However, if you've got to remind yourself to concentrate during an athletic contest, you're not concentrating on the event, but you are concentrating on "trying to concentrate" which only takes your mind off the performance that you want to concentrate on.

Another misconception about concentration is that the mind should never waver throughout the contest. This may be true in some, but not all, sports. Concentration varies in both intensity and duration. At certain times the intensity must be high (such as during the pitch in baseball) and at other times the intensity need not be as high.

The duration of concentration can vary as well. Some athletes concentrate on their sport throughout the entire contest while others have high degrees of concentration during actual play and break concentration entirely at other times. Yet, these athletes can be just as effective at concentrating as others.

Different styles of concentration are used by different athletes. An excellent comparison would be the different, yet very successful, styles perfected by Bjorn Borg versus John McEnroe in tennis. Borg's style is one of long-term, unwavering concentration throughout the match. McEnroe shouts at umpires and fans and often appears disgusted at himself and others at various times during a match. Yet, he can snap back to the task at hand and intensely concentrate on the game when needed without any apparent loss of effectiveness.

The key point to remember is that each person is different and you can develop your own successful style without emulating others.

TECHNIQUES TO IMPROVE CONCENTRATION

To be effective at concentrating means you are able to (1) alter the intensity of your concentration as needed, (2) alter the duration of your concentration as needed, and (3) change the focus of your concentration instantly to stay with the flow of the game.

Practicing the program outlined in this book is one way to improve concentration. Relaxation improves concentration because, during the techniques, you are concentrating intently to pick up the sensations that are difficult to perceive without concentrating. Throughout the four steps of the mental conditioning program, I have emphasized that you should not allow the mind to wander, even when deeply relaxed. This improves concentration because you must continually concentrate to monitor your level of alertness. In essence, when practicing all steps of the program you are practicing concentration.

Other techniques can also be used to improve concentration. The two presented here are simple to do and can be practiced in non-competitive situations. As you do these techniques remember that you must not allow your mind to wander. Do not get too relaxed and drift into sleep, but remain alert throughout the entire practice period. If your mind does wander, shorten the practice session.

Exhalation Counting

This technique is a variation of the Exhalation Exercise from Chapter 5. Assume a comfortable position (either lying down or sitting upright in a chair) and focus on your breathing cycle. You will count consecutively on each exhalation, one number per exhalation. On each inhalation you will repeat the word "In." Count from 1 to 10; then go back to one and begin over. The sequence will be as follows. "In" (as you inhale), "One" (as you exhale); "In, Two;" "In, Three;" and so on up to ten. Then begin again at one. Begin doing this technique for two to four minutes. With practice you will be able to go ten to fifteen minutes without losing count. Be sure to concentrate as you do the technique and do not count beyond ten. Also, do not allow the mind to drift as you get deeply relaxed.

Sequential Breathing

The Sequential Breathing Technique, a variation of the Sequential Relaxation Exercise from Chapter 5, is similiar to the Brief Body Scan IR Technique. In this variation, you will focus on a key sensation as you move through the body in the same sequence used during the Sequential Relaxation Exercise. As you practice, you train yourself to feel this sensation on one breath for each body part. For example, use the "sinking down" sensation as you go through the entire body in sequence and feel each body part "sinking down" on one breath. On each successive breath move to the next body part and feel that one "sinking down."

Use the following sequence as you move through the body: right foot and ankle, left foot and ankle, right lower leg (calf), left lower leg, right thigh, left thigh, buttocks and hips, trunk (including the shoulders), right arm and hand, left arm and hand; then, on one breath, feel the entire body "sinking down." After you have completed the entire sequence using the sensation of "sinking down," repeat it using the sensation of "heaviness." "Warmth" is another sensation to use. Start with "sinking down" because it is the easiest to feel. Add "heaviness" second, and, when you feel you can concentrate readily, add the sensation of "warmth" which is more difficult to feel and requires greater concentration to accomplish.

The key is to feel the sensation on one breath in each body part and then be able to change the focus of your concentration to a different body part for the next breath. This technique trains you to concentrate for longer periods of time; to concentrate more intensely as the sensations become more difficult to feel; and to change the focus of attention while continuing to concentrate, much like that which occurs during actual participation in sports.

Regaining Concentration
During a Contest

All athletes occasionally lose concentration during a contest. One of the things that separates good athletes from the not so good is the ability to regain concentration after it has been lost.

Concentration can be broken during a sporting contest in many ways. I have found the two most common reasons are: (1) breaks in the thought pattern because of distractions and (2) invading thoughts of failure.

Prevalent distractions in any athletic contest are crowd noise and movement along with distractions caused by your competitors. In fact, part of the strategy in many sports includes techniques to break the concentration of your opponents while they try to do likewise to you.

Thoughts of failure are also commonplace during competitions, especially for athletes with negative self-images. During stressful situations, invading thoughts of failure such as "What will my parents (friends, teammates, coaches, etc.) think of me if I miss this basket," often surface. Another common invading thought that can break concentration is the image of "what you want to avoid." Rather than focusing on getting a hit to tie the game, the thought that appears in this situation may be "I don't want to strike out".

Regardless of the reason for a break in concentration, regaining concentration quickly is often the difference between success and failure. Generally concentration is broken when the mind wanders from the present to either a past failure or to a future worry. The key to regaining concentration is to bring the mind back to the present — to the here and now.

THE PRESENT MOMENT TECHNIQUE

The Present Moment Technique incorporates several techniques presented in this book. Its goal is threefold: first, to bring the mind back to the present (and forget distracting thoughts about what happened in the past or could happen in the future); second, to relax the body (using an IR technique); and third, to mentally rehearse the Present Moment Rehearsal (which is discussed in the next section). Although this technique is discussed under the heading of Regaining Concentration, it can be used to heighten concentration and improve focusing as well.

Description

After losing concentration and identifying the need to regain it, do the following:

1. Look at something in the environment that has no relevance to the present situation, and study it for a period of time to clear your mind of worries. For example, look at the scoreboard and select a letter or a number and examine it in detail. Look at the color, the texture, the brightness. Or look at your hand, the ball, bat, or club — anything that will bring your mind to the present environment but in and of itself has no meaning.

2. Do an IR technique. Use the Brief Body Scan Technique, if you have the time, or the Deep Breath Technique allowing the exhalation phase of the breathing cycle to relax the body.

3. Do the Present Moment Rehearsal (described in the following section) if it is appropriate. This allows successful thoughts to fill your mind as you view what you want to have happen in the next moment or two.

Although the three steps look time-consuming, they can be done in 20 to 30 seconds if need be. To enhance your ability to perform this technique during actual competition, it should be practiced regularly. Perform this technique regularly during athletic practice sessions.

Mental Rehearsal During Competition

In many sports mental rehearsal of the skill you are about to perform can be done during the actual competition. If you are doing mental rehearsal during competition it usually has to be done relatively quickly just prior to the actual skill performance. The Present Moment Technique or variations of this technique can be adapted to most sports.

THE PRESENT MOMENT REHEARSAL

The Present Moment Rehearsal technique is performed during actual competition. It can be used by the basketball player just prior to a free throw, the golfer just prior to a shot, the tennis player prior to a serve, and the like.

Description

1. To do the Present Moment Rehearsal, begin by relaxing the body with an IR technique. One breath should be sufficient to calm the body.

2. Then, picture yourself performing the skill that you are about to do. As you visualize the performance (from within your body just as if you are performing the skill), feel the actual movements of the body kinesthetically. In addition, see the end result of the movement as you accomplish your goal.

For example, if you are shooting a putt in golf, exhale and calm the body, feel the shot and visualize the path of the ball as it rolls across the green and into the hole. If you can feel the movement and visualize the end result, the body will put into work the actual movements needed by both the nervous system and muscular system to accomplish the end goal. This concept was discussed and illustrated in Chapter 2 as you performed Chevereul's pendulum technique.

Using Imagery in Healing

The principles discussed throughout this book can be used to improve health. Research indicates that stress is a major culprit in the onset of illness, including infectious diseases such as the common cold and the flu. When the body is under chronic stress, which often occurs during a competitive season, susceptibility to nagging health problems increases. Therefore, learning stress control and regular relaxation is helpful in preventing illness.

In addition, research on the role of imagery and a positive attitude in the healing process is encouraging indeed. There is a scientific basis supporting the use of relaxation and mental imagery in the healing process. When an athlete is injured, one of the first steps in the healing process within the body is the need for increased circulation to the injured area. This increased blood flow removes waste products and brings nutrients so the healing process can begin.

Relaxation improves blood flow throughout the body by dilating the blood vessels. With training, and using certain relaxation techniques as well as imagery, you can learn to alter blood flow to certain body parts, including the injured site. This increased circulation aids the recovery and often shortens the healing process.

Body Breathing Techniques

Body breathing exercises allow you to relax specific body parts by combining relaxation techniques with imagery. These techniques can be used to control pain, remove tension, and increase circulation to specific sites. All body breathing exercises/techniques are based on the long breath technique which was developed by Dr. Beata Jencks. As the base technique, the long breath should be learned first.

THE LONG BREATH

Dr. Jencks designed the long breath technique to teach body breathing principles. While performing this technique, a person uses imagery to breathe in and out of various parts of the body.

Description

Perform a relaxation technique and allow the body to achieve a deeply relaxed state. Now, inhale through the nose. As you exhale, imagine, in a manner in which you are comfortable, the exhaled air flowing out through the bottom of your feet. On each exhalation, visualize or think about the air flowing down the trunk, the legs, and permit the air to flow out through the feet (either the bottoms of the feet or out the toes). Feel, sense, and experience any sensations that occur in the area of the feet.

Repeat the above sequence on each successive breathing cycle for several cycles.

SPECIFIC SITE RELAXATION

Specific Site Relaxation applies the principles learned in the Long Breath technique to a specific area of the body. For example, say that you have injured the lower back and would like to reduce the pain, remove tension in surrounding muscles, and improve circulation to the area to aid the healing process. The following description of Specific Site Relaxation adapts the technique to the lower back. You, of course, would substitute your injured site for the lower back as described in the exercise below.

Description

Perform basic relaxation until you are in a deeply relaxed state. Then, as you breathe in, imagine that the air is flowing into the body through the nose. Visualize the air streaming down through the trunk. As you exhale, imagine the air flowing out of the body in the lower back area. Imagine this same sequence on each successive breath and visualize, in any manner you choose, the air carrying the tensions and pains of the lower back out of the body. On each breath, feel the lower back becoming more and more relaxed, warm, and comfortable.

Maintaining Skill Level While Injured

When using relaxation and imagery for healing, remember to use the mental conditioning program to practice your skill level. Imagery can help maintain your skill level, even if you are unable to physically practice your sport.

The following example illustrates the importance of imagery in maintaining skill level while injured.

Several years ago a young woman javelin thrower set a national record of 156 feet in the semifinals of the national meet and placed second in the finals of the meet as a junior. During the summer she injured her rotator cuff muscle in her throwing arm. Since she was unable to throw during her senior year, she spent her practice time working on and perfecting her footwork. In addition, she practiced throwing the javelin mentally at least twice daily.

During her entire senior year she threw the javelin just five times. Her first throw took place at a major invitational meet; she won the meet with the throw. Her second throw of the season, in the conference tournament, qualified her for the conference finals. Her third throw of the season won the conference tournament for her. The fourth throw took place at the national tournament and qualified her for the national finals.

She took her fifth and final throw of the season in the finals of the national tournament and not only won the meet but also set a national meet record with a throw of 170 feet.

CHAPTER 11

STANDARD AUTOGENIC TRAINING

Standard Autogenic Training (SAT) is a technique developed by J.H. Schultz in Germany in the early 1900's.

The title of SAT itself is descriptive of the technique. Standard, meaning the basic technique (versus Advanced Autogenic Techniques); Autogenic, meaning "self induced"; and Training, meaning it is done on a regular basis. For our purposes that will mean it is done three or more times daily.

Benefits of SAT

SAT is a relaxation technique and will offer those benefits that can be derived from regular relaxation. SAT also offers additional benefits important in athletics. I consider it the best technique available for improving concentration – both duration and intensity. It is also the best I've seen for learning to shift concentration quickly while competing because, throughout the entire training period, you are practicing intense concentration as well as shifting concentration levels.

IMPLEMENTATION

SAT contains a total of six different exercises designed to train one's body and one's mind to respond to their wishes. Each phase of SAT gets progressively harder to perform and thus requires greater concentration. In addition, each phase is added to previous phases, and you are, therefore, more relaxed as you add each step. This means, that as you add steps, it will become more difficult for you to concentrate because you will have a greater tendency to allow your mind to wander or to drift into sleep. To achieve maximum benefits **do not allow your mind to wander at any time!!!**

The Six Week SAT Program

I suggest the following guidelines to achieve the maximum benefits from the time spent doing autogenic training:

1. Perform all three repetitions of SAT before you perform your mental training (i.e., positive affirmations, mental recall and mental rehearsal). Use the autogenic phrases for the relaxation component of your mental training program.

2. You can substitute the feeling for the phrase in SAT. For example, instead of stating "My right arm is heavy," you can feel the heaviness in the right arm instead. Even when you use the phrase in your mind, you should feel the sensation of heaviness on the exhalation.

3. Remain alert throughout each practice session. If at any time you are feeling too relaxed and cannot remain alert, or are too tired, stop, take a deep breath, flex/stretch and come back to an alert state before doing the mental training.

4. Feel the sensations that you are searching for on the **exhalation phase of your breathing cycle only.**

5. Log each practice session.

ATTENTION/CAUTION

Standard Autogenic Training is **not for everyone!** Many people consider SAT a form of self-hypnosis. Although most people view self-hypnosis as positive, it is not viewed that way by everyone. If you have any reservations at all regarding the technique, do not use it. Or, if you have any problems with it discontinue its use.

Keep in mind that SAT is not needed to derive the benefits of mental practice. The four-step MFW Program offers the techniques needed for success by itself. Advanced techniques such as SAT can add to the success of the program but are not needed to guarantee success.

SAT
Step One: Heaviness

Phrase to be used: "My _____ is heavy."

For six breaths (and six breaths only, not five or seven), say to yourself "My right arm is heavy." As you do so, you should feel the heaviness (on the exhalation phase of your breathing cycle) in your right arm. Time your phrase or thought with your breathing cycle so you can feel the heaviness in the right arm as you exhale.

On the seventh breath, switch your attention to your left arm and use the phrase, "My left arm is heavy." You then feel the heaviness in the left arm for a total of six breaths (or through the 12th breath).

You then move to the right leg for six breaths and then the left leg for the same, each time changing the phrases accordingly. Then you flex, stretch and open your eyes. Immediately, you repeat the entire sequence a second time, come out of it, and then repeat it a third time.

At the end of the third repetition you can perform your mental training (affirmations, recall and rehearsal).

SUGGESTIONS FOR SUCCESS:

1. Count each exhalation to make sure you're doing six breaths for each repetition. For example, "One, my right arm is heavy, two, my right arm is heavy, etc." After several days of practice, the counting will not be necessary. You will automatically stop after six breaths because five or seven will not "feel" right.

2. Concentrate so that you feel the heaviness on each breath. You can feel the heaviness anywhere in the limb. For example, you may feel it only in a fingertip or you may feel it in the entire hand or the entire limb. Even if you have trouble feeling heaviness or cannot feel it at all initially, **Do not go for any extra breaths, use six breaths only.**

3. When you begin to feel heaviness with ease, change the phrase to "My _____ is comfortably heavy."

TRAINING SEQUENCE: Week One

Each session includes the following:

First Repetition

"My right arm is heavy." 6 breaths
"My left arm is heavy." 6 breaths
"My right leg is heavy." 6 breaths
"My left leg is heavy." 6 breaths

Flex, stretch, and open your eyes.

Second And Third Repetitions

Repeat entire sequence above a second time and then repeat entire sequence a third time. Following the third repetition perform your mental training before coming out of the relaxed state.

SAT
Step Two: Warmth

Phrase to be used: "My _____ is warm."

Starting on the eighth day, you will shorten the time spent on heaviness and add warmth to the sequence. Warmth will be more difficult to feel but if you've practiced daily you will have no trouble feeling the warmth on the first day.

TRAINING SEQUENCE: Week Two

First Repetition

"My right arm is heavy." 1 breath
"My left arm is heavy." 1 breath
"My right leg is heavy." 1 breath
"My left leg is heavy." 1 breath
"My right arm is warm." 6 breaths
"My left arm is warm." 6 breaths

"My right leg is warm." 6 breaths
"My left leg is warm." 6 breaths

Flex, stretch, and open your eyes.

Second and Third Repetitions

Repeat above and follow the third repetition with mental practice.

SAT
Step Three: Heartbeat

Phrase to be used: "My heart is strong and regular" or "My heartbeat is strong and calm." While you repeat this phrase, feel your heart beating in your chest.

During this step, the previous steps are going to be shortened. Heaviness should be felt in both arms on one breath, then in both legs on the second breath. This requires you to focus your attention on each arm very quickly during that one breath. Warmth will also be shortened to one breath per limb.

TRAINING SEQUENCE: Week Three

First Repetition

"My arms are heavy." 1 breath
"My legs are heavy." 1 breath
"My right arm is warm." 1 breath
"My left arm is warm." 1 breath
"My right leg is warm." 1 breath
"My left leg is warm." 1 breath
"My heartbeat is strong and regular." 6 breaths

Flex, stretch, and open your eyes.

Second and Third Repetitions

Repeat above sequence and practice your mental training techniques following the third repetition.

SAT
Step Four: Breathing

Phrase to be used: "It breathes me." Passively observe your breathing cycle and breathing rate while you exhale.

The "It" is your body. Just allow your body to breathe by itself while you focus on the breathing. This will carry you into a very deeply relaxed state. As you add this step, you will once again shorten the previous steps. Each repetition will now require much less time but increased concentration on your part. For example, as you say, "My arms and legs are heavy," you move your mind and attention from right arm to left arm to right leg to left leg, feeling heaviness in each – **all during one exhalation.** Then immediately move to warmth and do the same for warmth. You are now feeling in one breath what was taking you 24 breaths early in the training.

TRAINING SEQUENCE: Week Four

First Repetition

"My arms and legs are heavy." 1 breath
"My arms and legs are warm." 1 breath
"My heartbeat is strong and regular." 1 breath
"It breathes me." 6 breaths

Flex, stretch, and open your eyes.

Second and Third Repetitions

Repeat above a second and third time. Following the third repetition, perform your mental training.

SAT
Step Five: Internal Warmth

Phrase to be used: "My solar plexus is warm." Feel warmth in the internal portion of the trunk of your body (behind the heart, in front of the spine).

All previous steps will be shortened to one breath each when Step Five is added. As you repeat the statement or think the phrase, feel the warmth for a total of six breaths for each repetition of SAT. This will follow the previous four steps during each practice session as illustrated below.

TRAINING SEQUENCE: Week Five

First Repetition

"My arms and legs are heavy." 1 breath
"My arms and legs are warm." 1 breath
"My heartbeat is strong and regular." 1 breath
"It breaths me." 1 breath
"My solar plexus is warm." 6 breaths

Flex, stretch, and open your eyes.

Second and Third Repetitions

Repeat the above sequence a second and then a third time. Following the third repetition, perform your mental training.

SAT
Step Six: Cool Forehead

Phrase to be used: "My forehead is cool." Feel coolness on the forehead while you repeat this phrase on the exhalation. (*NOTE:* I have found that this step is uncomfortable to some people. If the cool forehead bothers you, disregard this last step and complete your training at this point.)

TRAINING SEQUENCE: Week Six

First Repetition

"My arms and legs are heavy." 1 breath

"My arms and legs are warm." 1 breath
"My heartbeat is strong and regular." 1 breath
"It breaths me." 1 breath
"My solar plexus is warm." 1 breath
"My forehead is cool." 6 breaths

Flex, stretch, and open your eyes.

Second and Third Repetitions

Repeat above sequence following the third repetition with mental training techniques.